"This book is as insightful, unconventional, and original as its author. It will change how you see things, and it will change what you do." **From the Foreword by Andrew McAfee Principal Research Scientist at MIT and author of** *Enterprise 2.0*

"Euan is one of the top thinkers in the world about how the web ACTUALLY works, as opposed to how the trendy guru types like to PRETEND it works. Read everything he's written, is my advice." **Hugh MacLeod, cartoonist**

"Euan has not only been there and done it, he has also thought profoundly about it. Highly recommended." **Dave Snowden, Chief Scientific Officer, Cognitive Edge**

"One of the best minds in the world just to be around. Highly recommended." **Thomas Power, Founder and CEO, Ecademy**

"A clear explanation of how flatter structures, self-organising teams and vanishing boundaries can be good for business, from one of the sharpest thinkers on the merits of social business, knowledge management and radical transparency." **Richard Sambrook, Global Vice Chairman, Edelman**

"From the title of the book, to chapter headings, to the actual words, Euan's positive fun-loving personality and forward-thinking passion for "making organizations better" shine through. With humour and directness, he shares insights and ideas about what's possible in the workplace, the technologies that can enable effectiveness, and the people who will make it happen. Well done Euan!" **Jane Dysart, KMWorld Conference Chair, Dysart & Jones Associates**

"In this easy-to-read yet insightful book, Euan brings the thoughts he has been sharing on his blog together and invites readers to have a dance with him, to learn, practice and submerge ourselves in the steps to make 2.0 work. Enjoyable read!" **Dr Bonnie Cheuk, Director Global Head of Knowledge & Collaboration, Citi**

"Euan's voice – thoughtful, humorous, humane, cautiously optimistic – is distinctive among the general babble about social media and web 2.0. It cuts through the confusion, making practical suggestions that can be acted on quickly, but also, in a down-to earth way, drawing you into a bigger and more important conversation about why all this matters. And it does." **Dr Matthew Shaw, Curator, US Collections, The British Library**

"In a world full of phoney social media 'gurus' it's hard to find people who actually know what they're talking about. Euan Semple is the most pioneering, visionary thinker of our times and probably the very best at explaining the web in ways we can all understand. Euan was a massive influence on our social business approach which now sees thousands of people working in a whole new way around the world. This refreshing book makes his thoughts and insights available to all. An inspiring must-read for anyone serious about doing business in today's world." **Nick Crawford, Social Business Strategist, Bupa**

"Euan has not only mastered the fine art of setting the stage and letting work of real value emerge through social means, he is also capable of teaching others the fine art of allowing more to come about than just what was planned. This book takes his wisdom, his learnings and his brilliant way of expressing it and puts it in a form to allow organizations to proceed under their own steam. Read it, discuss it and seize the opportunity to unleash your organization." **Bruce A Stewart, Director, The iSchool Institute, Faculty of Information, University of Toronto**

"A thoughtful, intelligent book for managers and executives. Euan explores the real meaning of democracy and shows why it's a great model for modern corporations. He explicitly reveals the differences between anarchy, libertarianism and genuine democracy. He reminds us that the essence of democracy is personal responsibility. When everyone in the organisation takes responsibility for his or her actions, the organisation – and the world around it – becomes a far better place." **Mike Barlow, co-author, *The Executive's Guide to Enterprise Social Media Strategy* and *Partnering with the CIO***

"Euan has a knack for bringing clarity and cohesion to the disparate elements of what we broadly term social collaboration. It is easy to get stimulated by the possibilities of interactivity but not so easy to productively introduce those elements inside the business firewalls. Euan provides that roadmap and more. He is a pioneer in blazing the path . . ." **Stephen Collesano Ph.D., Senior Vice President, Global Research, ACE Group**

"The book covers an incredibly comprehensive range of aspects of our digital lives. Each chapter inspired me to a number of new ideas I will be spending the next few months exploring further and hopefully soon applying!" **Christer Holloman, Chairman, First Tuesday UK**

"Euan demystifies many of the notions associated with the frequently over-hyped term 'social media', offers the reader real-world and pragmatic guidance and shares his vision for a better future. If you want to understand the forces that have the potential to transform businesses, and the way we all work – read this book." **Matthew Hanwell, HR Director, Communities and Social Media, Nokia**

"If poetry is the art of finding words for things that are difficult to express or would otherwise be left untold, then Euan must be the poet par excellence of the social media and collaboration world. Anybody who is working in social media is ultimately an advocate and as such is in a constant struggle to find the right words to articulate the need for change, to describe what they are doing in plain terms, to demystify the technology and bring the attention back to the human element. Euan has the unique talent to provide the struggling social media evangelist with a vocabulary that is stripped of any hype or pomposity, and crystallises in memorable quotes, questions and challenges that they face in their daily work. What they felt or knew for a long time but could not possibly articulate is put in front of them with disarming simplicity. It is hard to describe what empowering effect finding the right words can have. I am thinking of classic Euan aphorisms like "social media adoption happens one person at a time, and for their reasons, not yours", which has for long been a poster in my office and I have been endlessly using in trainings. *Organizations Don't Tweet, People Do* has already become one of my favourites. With this book, the social media advocate's struggle for words comes to an end. My gratitude goes to Euan for, once again, telling the untold." **Giulio Quaggiotto, Practice Leader, Knowledge and Innovation, UNDP (views are personal, not UNDP)**

ORGANIZATIONS DON'T TWEET, PEOPLE DO

A Manager's Guide to the Social Web

EUAN SEMPLE

A John Wiley & Sons, Ltd., Publication

This edition first published 2012
© 2012 Euan Semple

Registered office
John Wiley & Sons Ltd, The Atrium, Southern Gate, Chichester, West Sussex, PO19 8SQ, United Kingdom

For details of our global editorial offices, for customer services and for information about how to apply for permission to reuse the copyright material in this book please see our website at www.wiley.com.

Wiley publishes in a variety of print and electronic formats and by print-on-demand. Some material included with standard print versions of this book may not be included in e-books or in print-on-demand. If this book refers to media such as a CD or DVD that is not included in the version you purchased, you may download this material at http://booksupport.wiley.com. For more information about Wiley products, visit www.wiley.com.

Designations used by companies to distinguish their products are often claimed as trademarks. All brand names and product names used in this book are trade names, service marks, trademarks or registered trademarks of their respective owners. The publisher is not associated with any product or vendor mentioned in this book. This publication is designed to provide accurate and authoritative information in regard to the subject matter covered. It is sold on the understanding that the publisher is not engaged in rendering professional services. If professional advice or other expert assistance is required, the services of a competent professional should be sought.

Library of Congress Cataloging-in-Publication Data

Semple, Euan.
  Organizations don't tweet, people do : a managers guide to the social Web / Euan Semple.
     p. cm.
   ISBN 978-1-119-95055-4 (hardback)
1. Online social networks.   2. Management.   I. Title.
   HM742.S45 2012
   302.3068–dc23

                                        2011046736

A catalogue record for this book is available from the British Library.

ISBN 978-1-119-95055-4 (hbk) ISBN 978-1-119-95130-8 (ebk)
ISBN 978-1-119-95131-5 (ebk) ISBN 978-1-1199-5132-2 (ebk)

Set in 10/13.5pt Caecilia by Toppan Best-set Premedia Limited
Printed in Great Britain by TJ International Ltd, Padstow, Cornwall, UK

CONTENTS

FOREWORD

Euan Semple was a rumour to me before he was a col-
league. In the middle of the new millennium's first
decade, as I was trying to understand what if anything
was really going on with this 'Web 2.0' meme and what if
anything it might mean to organizations outside the tech
sector, I started to hear about a bloke who had answers.
And he had them not because he had conducted studies or
invented cool new digital tools, but as a result of his work
actually accomplishing the kinds of technology-enabled
business improvements I thought might theoretically, one
day, be possible.

Over time the rumours coalesced into a fuzzy but intrigu-
ing picture. While working at the BBC, Euan had become
profoundly frustrated with the organization's tools, processes, and approaches for gathering and sharing its own
knowledge, whether in printed form or lodged in the heads
of the people who worked there. He realized the sad truth

of former HP CEO Lew Platt's comment: "If only HP knew what HP knows, we'd be three times as productive."

But instead of buying one more piece of KM or portal software or hosting one more conference, Euan had thrown out the playbook and started doing some weird things. Like putting in place a forum where people could ask any question they liked to the BBC as a whole, without much if any filtering or specifying where the question should 'go' to be answered. Like launching this capability with very little fanfare, instead of as much as possible. And like trusting that word would get around to the people at the Beeb, and that they could be trusted to use it appropriately and professionally. And the rumours were clear about what happened next: *it worked*.

So clearly, I needed to talk to this guy. I got my first chance at a session in 2007 where I was a panelist and Euan was in the audience. During the question and answer portion he identified himself, and then made it clear to me (and everyone else in the room) that our positions should have been reversed that day. And he did it not by being combative or a know-it-all, but instead by demonstrating his experience and insight every time he spoke.

Those qualities have carried through in every interaction I've had with him since, and everything of his I've read, including this book. And in the years I've known him I've learned one more thing about Euan: he's passionate about making things better. The truly wonderful thing about the movement he and I are interested in – call it the social web, or social business, or Enterprise 2.0, or whatever – is that it makes two important things better at once. It improves business outcomes, and it improves the work lives of people within businesses because it gives them a voice, and a chance to manifest what Nelson Mandela calls their "spark of genius."

This book is as insightful, unconventional, and original as its author. I'm thrilled to see that he's taken the time to write down what he's learned so that the rest of us can benefit from it. This book will change how you see things, and it will change what you do.

Thanks, Euan, for writing it.

Andrew McAfee
Principal Research Scientist at MIT and
author of Enterprise 2.0

INTRODUCTION

Who is this book for? Well, it is really for anyone who works and is interested in how the web and the Internet are affecting the way we work now and will do in the future. It is not a "how to" book nor, I hope, is it a cyber-utopian vision of the future. There are enough of both of those around already. I prefer to think of it as a collection of ideas that individually or together can make the web more understandable and useful in the world of work. Whether you have "got it" already or not there can be little doubt that the impact of the web in the workplace is increasing. More people use it more of the time to do more stuff. Our workplaces are lagging behind what we can do at home and the pressure is increasingly on us to keep up. How do you do this as an individual and as an organization? Hopefully the ideas in this book will help you to work that out.

You can read this book from start to finish or you can read the chapters individually if you like. Browse the index and dip into topics that catch your eye. Each chapter is intended to be just long enough for a visit to the executive restroom . . . Enough to help convey the essence of an aspect of the web at work. Enough to whet your appetite to get involved, or to help you understand what other people are going on about and maybe encourage you to let them do more.

I read an inordinate amount of management, productivity, and self help books. I know the kind that have worked for me and those that haven't. The ones that work pique my interest. Suggest things to me rather than lecture at me. Give me a sense of possibility rather than a sense of foreboding. So I wrote the book with this in mind, to help you understand the potential of the web at work. To help you gain traction and to engage others in the changes you are trying to bring about. It is not a management textbook nor is it a self help book, it is somewhere in between.

I don't talk about technology much in this book. It is more about what technology is enabling rather than which tool does what. However I have included at the end an overview of the currently available types of tools for those of you not already familiar with the technologies available. Hopefully this will be enough to give you a sense of what I am talking about when I refer throughout the book to "these tools".

I am not saying that the social web is for everyone. You can take it or leave it. You or your organization may not feel ready for it now. I do believe that it offers possibilities to everyone and its use in business is ultimately inevitable. However people have to adopt it for their own reasons and they can't be forced. Those who are successful at deploying social tools in business tend to be good at enticing people into their use and try to make them relevant and useful to as many people as possible. I have tried to do the same in this book. It is like a commonplace book of ideas, trinkets, or nuggets to draw you in. Ideas to make you feel more capable. Practices to make you more effective. I hope you enjoy reading it.

1

WE ALL NEED TO GROW UP

We are used to thinking of the world in terms of mass. Big things like nation states, religions, society, the media. We are used to expecting those big things to look after us and protect us. But the Internet splits those up and breaks them apart. It is made up of networks of individuals, each with their own voice. If we are going to survive the changes we need to see in our institutions we need to help them find that voice. We need to help them grow up.

There is something inherently personal about the social tools we will be talking about in this book. From the early days of blogging, when there was much talk of authenticity and finding your voice, to the amazing openness and transparency being exhibited in Facebook by unbelievable numbers of people, the emphasis has been on the individual and their particular take on the world around them. This is the first time that we have each had our own capacity to broadcast our ideas on a global scale in this way and for virtually no cost.

The patterns we are seeing in our use of the Internet are all part of the ongoing and inevitable ebb and flow of power between the individual and society. Whether it is the state, or the multinational corporation, or the churches of our major religions – between which there are more similarities than most people like to admit – how we relate to the large and powerful bodies that influence so much of our lives is what is at stake here. Your IT department is locking down access to Facebook and the state attempting to legislate to protect us from ourselves. There is a seemingly inevitable tendency for those in power to want to close things down and wield authority to maintain the status quo. At the same time individuals, of whatever political or even religious persuasion, embrace the ability the web gives them to have a voice.

There has been nothing like this since the printing press and its impact will be on a similar scale. The printing press, and the easy access to ideas that it enabled, fuelled the Reformation in Europe and this was driven by the desire to be able to read the Bible in languages other than the official Latin. The church went to the extreme of burning people in their attempts to resist this process so we can be pretty sure it was as much about power as it was about piety. The courage of those who embraced this new freedom to think for themselves ultimately led to the Enlightenment and to our modern world view. If, as many of us believe, the web is taking us on the next step in this journey of self-expression and self-determination, where we are even cutting out the publishers of our words, it's likely that it will have the same profound long-term effect on our culture and our philosophies as did the printing press.

The alternatives to maintaining the familiar structures and behaviours of modern society are portrayed as beyond the pale. Words like chaos and anarchy are used to create the impression that without the grown-ups looking after us catastrophe would inevitably ensue. In the world of work, fitting in with corporate culture is seen as necessary and anyone straying too far from the norm is soon pulled back. Thinking too much is seen as a bad thing in many work-places and "having ideas above your station" a frequent admonishment. I am not pretending that people don't behave badly or that companies don't have to manage their relationships with customers and stakeholders carefully, but in doing so they severely limit what is possible. Will chaos really ensue if we don't keep a lid on things? Is this only true because we have been trained to act like children and expect others to make our decisions for us?

There is always a tendency to blame the sins of the pre-vious generation on the behaviour of the new one. Whether it is television, rock and roll, or the Internet, it is all too easy to demonize the new and unfamiliar and to blame it for society's ills. Those in authority are prone to knee-jerk reactions when things go wrong – to blame what is only understood by a minority and to prey on the fears of the majority. We see this in corporations' paranoia about Face-book and governments blaming social tools for upheavals in society. But they are all just tools. Tools used by people to do things they care about. If we are not happy with what we are using those tools for then we need to think hard about what we deem important.

We will only be able to take full advantage of the networked world if we grow up, think for ourselves, and take responsibility for our lives and our actions. I am not naïve. I know that, at least to begin with, truly thinking for yourself and saying what you think with any degree of authenticity is a big ask. It may never happen for many people. There may just be too much at stake and too much to take into account for a politician or someone in a corporate setting to really be authentic. But I am hopeful. There are enough examples already where people have managed to tread that line. Managed to be real, to have a personality, and yet at the same time acknowledge the fact that they are "representing" a sector of society or a multinational corporation. It can be done.

Things to remember:

- Social tools are personal. They rely on individuals like you and me finding our voice.
- The Internet, like the printing press, is part of the ongoing process of humanity growing up.
- Power is shifting from institutions and corporations to networks and individuals.
- Chaos needn't be the only alternative to our current ways of controlling society.
- We need to grow up and take responsibility for our views and their impact.

2

TEN STEPS TO SUCCESS
WITH TECHNOLOGY

The focus of this book is deliberately *not* on technology. What we are talking about is much more important than that. But there is a technological basis for what is happening and one of the biggest challenges is to approach this new and unfamiliar set of tools in the most productive way. This chapter lays out a few principles and ten practical steps you can take to make your use of technology more productive and less painful.

For several reasons I have deliberately avoided talking too much about technology in this book. Firstly, it is too easy to dismiss what is happening as technological – to label it "digital" – and to miss the real point – the changes we are seeing are cultural. Cultural changes that were happening anyway and the web has simply helped to speed them up. This isn't a technological revolution followed by social change, but a social revolution made easier by technological change. People's attitudes to work and their employers were changing anyway. The stability of the permanent contract and the job for life was broken by the organizations themselves. People becoming less loyal was due to a growing lack of trust and increased need for independence – not people having access to Facebook! We can no longer rely on security of employment and more of us are aware of the possibility of taking responsibility for our own destinies. These changes were not brought about by technology – they came about as a result of the cracks appearing in the corporate mindset and our increased willingness to see the world differently.

The second reason for not talking more about technology is that it is a distraction. It is easy to get drawn into, and ground down by, endless conversations about this or that technological widget or to be seduced by yet another vendor promising you the earth. If you end up chasing the next shiny thing, or fixing the tarnished last one, you will have less energy and attention to focus on what really matters, which is the culture change and people. For many of us, using these tools will become an intrinsic part of everything we do and seeing it as alien or even novel means people haven't really "got it" yet. In fact it has become a warning sign to me when people say "Oh yes we do digital" because the word digital connotes "other". "It is not me who does it but others", or "it is not really what we do but an add-on".

The final reason not to be drawn into too much focus on tools is to keep things out of the hands of technologists as much as possible. Some of them aren't so bad, and some of them are re-inventing themselves, but most of those responsible for technology in most organizations have little experience of the tools that we are talking about and even less interest in what they enable. The goal of conventional IT has been to manage information in structured ways that reflect the business models of their organizations. The loose, networked, unpredictable environment generated by social tools is a considerable challenge to them. Indeed if there is a single biggest block to making social media happen encountered by my clients in large organizations it is their IT department.

So with those caveats in mind here are ten ideas about the tools that are worth keeping in mind as you begin to introduce them.

1. **Have a variety of tools rather than a single system.** Not everyone sees the world the same way or has the same needs so mixing up different tools with different strengths allows people to find one that works for them. Avoid single platforms like the plague.
2. **Don't have a clear idea where you are headed.** The more fixed you are in your aspirations for your ecology the less likely you are to achieve them. Be prepared to go where people's use of the tools takes you and enjoy the ride.
3. **Follow the energy.** Watch where the energy in the system is and try to copy the factors that generated it. Get others interested in why energy emerges and they will want some of it themselves.
4. **Be strategically tactical.** You can have an overall strategy of behaving in certain ways depending on how your ecology develops. It is possible to sell this as a strategy to those who need strategies.
5. **Keep moving, stay in touch, and head for the high ground.** Keep doing things, keep talking about what

you are doing and why, and have a rough idea of where the high ground is.

6. **Build networks of people who care.** Don't try to manage your ecology by committee but cultivate communication and trust between those who care that it works and have the commitment to do something about it – whoever they are and whatever their role.

7. **Be obsessively interested.** Notice everything that happens and consider why. Tell great stories about what you are observing.

8. **Use the tools to manage the tools.** Blog about what is going on with your corporate blogging, ask questions in your forum about security, tweet when something is changing in your ecology and ask people why it is interesting.

9. **Laugh when things go wrong.** If you are pushing limits and exploring new territory things will occasionally blow up in your face. Having a sense of humour and enjoyment of the absurd will help you stay sane.

10. **Unleash Trojan Mice.** Don't do big things or spend loads of money. Set small, nimble things running and see where they head.

I want to make one last comment on technology that is going to sound a little contradictory. While what is happening is not about the tools, it is about the underlying characteristics of the Internet and the web. The power of what is happening is based on the humble hyperlink – the ability to write a bit of code that allows one bit of text to link to another. I often think that what all these tools are really about is teaching people to use this link. Whether it is pointing in a forum to the thing that worked last time, linking in Facebook to the person we consider worth talking to, or blogging about the latest great bit of information on the web – we all use the humble link to point to things we think are important and worthy of note.

Given its importance we need to learn at least the basics of why this works the way it does. Tinker and be curious. Lift the lid on a web page and work out how it was constructed. Copy bits of it you like and use them yourself. Roll your sleeves up and get your hands dirty. Even if you do end up getting someone else to do your technology for you, you still need to know enough to know what you are buying from them. I see so many people getting charged large sums of money to have web tools set up or built for them when they could do the work themselves for practically nothing. It is important for everyone to have a grasp of some of the underlying principles that are enabling this revolution. Increasingly the code that underlies tools like Google and Facebook affects what we can and can't do with our lives. Read Larry Lessig's wonderful book *Code and Other Laws of Cyberspace* to appreciate why this all matters and why you should understand it. Code is about knowledge and knowledge is the source of power. If the real knowledge of how all of this works is in the hands of too small a group of people – even if it is your IT department – then we won't get the wonderful technological future that we deserve.

Things to remember:

- What we are seeing is a cultural change rather than a technological one.
- The Internet and the web are speeding up and enabling these cultural changes.
- Don't get drawn into too much detail, or too much expense, with the technology.
- Conventional technologists can find the web challenging – don't be too limited by their view of things.
- Remember the ten points on how to deploy the tools.
- Become interested in how links work, roll your sleeves up and tinker with code. Just enough to grasp what is going on!

3

THE ULTIMATE IN DEMOCRACY

We mostly run our businesses in a top down, centralized manner with a small group calling most of the shots. If the democratic process is deemed good enough for nation states why shouldn't it offer a new approach to running our businesses?

Someone once called me "an organizational anarchist" and I have to admit I was quite chuffed at the description and took it as a compliment. Wikipedia's entry on anarchy says:

> Anarchy (from Greek: ἀναρχία anarchía, "without ruler") may refer to any of several political states, and has been variously defined by sources. Most often, the term "anarchy" describes the simple absence of publicly recognized government or enforced political authority. When used in this sense, anarchy may or may not imply political disorder or lawlessness within a society. In another sense, anarchy may not refer to a complete lack of authority or political organization, but instead refer to a social state characterized by absolute direct democracy.
>
> Sourced from Wikipedia.org at http://en.wikipedia.org/wiki/Anarchy (http://creativecommons.org/licenses/by-sa/3.0/)

This is a long way from the modern picture of anarchists in black hoodies rioting in our streets but considering democracy in business produces the same reaction of horror. What I am talking about here is not complete free reign for individuals – the extremes of libertarianism do as much damage as the extremes of anarchism. We can't all look out for number one without any concern for our fellow man. What I am more interested in is the possibility of all of us taking full responsibility for ourselves and those around us – the ultimate in democracy, not the absence of it. Not chaos or man reverting to the status of beasts, but each person taking responsibility for their own thoughts and actions. "Before thought". Without ideology or dogma. Having to work out what we think and what is right and wrong from scratch. From our own resources. This would be hard work. It would be harder work than doing what we are told to do or thinking what we are told to think. This is what I will be talking about throughout this book. "Organizations don't tweet, people do" might as well be "Organizations don't think, people do".

No one is saying it is easy or without risk. You can't just pull out of a system on which people have become dependent, on which you have made them dependent, without first giving them some support. Once, when I was talking at a conference in Denmark, I started my keynote in an unusual way in order to make this point. I arranged with the chairman that when he introduced me I would not come onto the stage as expected but would be sitting in the audience. When it came to the moment, he announced me with great fanfare, people clapped expectantly – and then nothing. There was an empty stage and silence. People started to look around to see what was happening and some of them looked annoyed. I then started talking into my lapel microphone, in my normal speaking voice and said "That doesn't feel very comfortable does it?" Even more people looked around to see where this voice was coming from – who was this person behaving oddly? And even more of them looked even more annoyed. I then said "This is how people are going to feel when those who manage them, who have been assumed would act a certain way, start to act very differently." As I was saying this I was walking towards the stage and people looked visibly relieved as I started to play the role that they had all expected of me.

We have long assumed that the military idea of command and control, where those in authority have direct control over the actions of those under them, is the way we should run our organizations. The trouble is that even the military have mostly given up this way of looking at the world with autonomous, self-directing teams being more the norm in modern warfare.

Giving up on these assumptions is not easy. When command and control managers stop commanding and controlling, it is very disconcerting and not a pleasant feeling at first. But it is what is already happening around us. More of us than ever before are questioning our institutions and the way they function. People are starting to think more for themselves and seeking alternatives to the structure of the organization chart and apparent security of the salaried job for life. More of us are working out how to think entrepreneurially whether inside organizations or not. This shift in thinking is not just a result of the web. Attitudes were changing anyway, but the web is giving us the tools to do this new job of organizing ourselves – whatever form that takes.

Now here is a radical idea. As democracy faces the twin challenges of younger generations apparently disengaging from the electoral process and large corporations having a global influence that is less and less easy to draw under democratic control – how about moving democracy inside the firewall instead of outside it? Rather than trying to control the actions of corporations, non-government institutions, or even the government itself, through externally enforced rules and regulations decided upon on our behalf by our appointed representatives – what if we did it ourselves directly? What if there was a way for each of us to have our say inside the organizations we mostly work for instead of outside it? If we had lively and extensive internal online networks where we could collectively influence the decisions made at higher levels could we avoid some of the more damaging and self-serving corporate and institutional decisions? If enough of us went "Nah" could we have avoided Enron or the mortgage crash?

Is this naïve fantasy? Is this politically motivated radicalism? No – it is just my thoughts based on my experience both of life as a manager in a large organization and having spent twenty years on the web. It seems like a no brainer. It feels like where we are headed and it feels good. This is why I go on so much about people thinking hard and sharing what they think. This sort of anarchic, self-organizing system won't work unless people do the hard work of thinking for themselves.

The word organization shares the same root as organism and organic. We know from nature how complex self-directed systems work – in fact we are one ourselves. Our bodies are amazingly complex systems with individual cells that know their role and work in relation to the cells around them without control from some active central authority. We don't have to think about the important stuff like breathing – it does it itself. What if organizations could be the same? What if, even imperfectly, even partially, we had an organic rather than a machine metaphor in mind when we turned up for work in the mornings?

Things to remember:

■ Anarchy has had a bad press. What is not to like about the ultimate in democracy?
■ Our societies are changing around us along with our attitudes to our institutions.
■ These changes were happening anyway but the web is speeding them up.
■ If democracy works for nation states why not use it as a way of governing institutions from the inside?
■ If it is not working for nation states could we try to make it work from within our institutions?
■ The only way this will work is if we all learn to think for ourselves and look after each other.

4

LEAVING A TRACE

We would all like to make our mark on the world but for most of us this has been an unlikely hope. What we know and what we have learned from our work has been largely kept to ourselves. Until now.

Let's face it – most of us pass through a day, a month, perhaps even a whole career at work, without leaving much of a trace. We might write emails and reports but most of these get buried in the sea of information produced in the day to day of modern work and get stored on computer servers in "repositories" never to be seen again. When we leave our organizations, or even move between departments, there is usually little to indicate what we did, why, and what the point was.

It was with the ultimate irony that in the week that I left the BBC I found myself being asked to take part in a senior level meeting to discuss "how to prevent knowledge leaving the organization". However, unlike most other people leaving at the time, I did leave a trace. All of the blog posts, forum conversations, and wiki contributions I had made over the previous eight years or so were still there, and would continue to be available as long as the systems were left running. Indeed, unlike the usual traces left in formal business documentation, these online conversations contained much more of me, what I thought, what and how I decided, and what I cared about. I had, in other words, left a trace of my passing.

Much has been made of the business benefits of "knowledge retention". Organizations have instigated various practices to achieve this lofty aspiration, from exit interviews to "knowledge capture" exercises, but if these are done at all they usually happen after the event and are often done by third parties or written in a sanitized third person style. Most projects close without leaving much of a trace. Even if they are written up, any documentation produced tends to be formal and very limited in its scope. Even after action reviews more often than not pass on what you want others to see rather than all the messy, gutsy stuff that it really took to make the project happen.

In contrast to all of these conventional methods, what if you were creating your legacy as you worked? If you run your project on a wiki, discuss what is working, or not, on a forum, or write your interpretation of what you are doing on a blog, then all of that contextual richness is captured. Not captured in the usual knowledge management sense as dry business stuff stored in a knowledge coffin, but lively first person narrative, revealed as it is being thought through and worked out.

Blogging is very powerful in this context. There is something about its journal form that is current, engaging, and thoughtful. Even as an individual it is valuable to be able to get down in writing what is on your mind. To be able to look back and reflect on a particular series of events, or period in your working life, can afford valuable insights into what you did, why, and what you might learn for the future. These are traces. They are straggling paths – sometimes well worn paths – that lead hither and thither but give a real sense of place. The more well worn the path, the more valuable. Even if you have said the same things over and over, that too is interesting and valuable. What has obsessed you? What preyed heavily on your mind?

I hope you never have to be involved in anything as unpleasant as an industrial tribunal but if you do, having kept a journal could be invaluable – especially one written in public. What better way to show that you had nothing to hide and were doing things with the best of intentions? The flip side of course of leaving a trace is when you don't want to. When you have done something wrong, or screwed up, or are in the middle of doing something you know you shouldn't. This is where the public disclosure aspect of leaving a trace is more problematic. All corporations these days have an obligation to retain evidence of their written communication and with the growth of more social and chatty tools this creates issues of confidentiality. There are clearly times, and certain contexts, in which we can't afford to be totally open about everything, but even in these situations it is possible to capture the essence and the learning from a situation without compromising security or confidentiality.

The bottom line on security is if you don't want someone to read what you have written, don't write it on a computer. Easy to say, and easy to dismiss as unreasonable, but true nonetheless. One of the staggering things about the wikileaks exposures of US government files was the naïvety of some of those writing the email exchanges. Did they not realize that someone else would always be able to read their exchanges, even if only their own IT people? So think hard about what you are doing and what you are willing, or are able, to say about it. Be prepared to stand by what you think. Stand up for your ideas and your opinions. Leave a mark – literally. Let the world know why you did what you did and what you were thinking while you did it.

In contrast to the usual interpretation of "knowledge is power" – which means hoarding it and only giving it out occasionally – increasingly, the opposite is true. If you are not sharing it and letting it move around freely, you might as well not have your knowledge. It is only valuable if it is going somewhere – if it is flowing and being shared. It is like money. Think of all the movement-related words we apply to money – currency, transfer, exchange, etc. Knowledge is like any other form of value – it has to be moving to be valuable. Leaving your mark, leaving a trace is such a positive thing to do, both for yourself and your organization. It might not feel like it as you cautiously write down your first thoughts on your blog, but the effort to do so is motivated by the possibility, no matter how unlikely, that someone some time will read it. You are giving them access to your thoughts, and this is an act of generosity. The more we all open up and share our thinking, leaving a trace of our passing, the more we will all learn.

Things to remember:

- Most of us leave little indication of what we know when we leave a department or organization.
- Informal tools, used in the process of carrying out your work, are the best, and most painless, way to share what you know with those who might follow you.
- Even in situations where being open is difficult, we have to share as much as we can.
- Knowledge has to be shared to have value.

5

EVOLUTION ON STEROIDS

The web and social tools are all about learning. Learning about ourselves, learning about the world around us and learning from each other. In amongst the trivia there are very real opportunities to learn more – and faster – than we have ever had available to us before. It is like evolution on steroids.

Research has consistently shown that people prefer to learn from each other. In fact it is also showing nowadays that we are more likely to trust information from peers than we are from authorities. So what does this mean for how we learn at work? How do you tap into the accumulated knowledge of the people you work for, or indeed the companies you buy from, so that you learn faster and make better decisions? How do you make the most of this shift in trust from authorities to individuals and networks?

The trouble with much corporate training is that it is still very focused around delivering "content" to people who then "consume" it rather than about informed conversations between people learning from each other and passing on the latest knowledge. Even universities and management colleges are struggling to know what to do with our ever increasing ability to learn from each other. What is the role of a lecturer or a teacher when we have more facts than we know what to do with but risk understanding less and less? In the world of commerce, communication with customers is still focused on selling to them and maintaining a brand image rather than helping them really understand our products and learn how they can make a difference in their lives.

Imagine if this was different. Imagine if inside your business everyone blogged. If everyone thought hard about what they did, what worked and why and then wrote about it in a way that piqued the interest of those around them facing the same challenges or affected by their work. Imagine if your experts developed their understanding by writing thoughtfully about their skills and then shared them with their colleagues. Imagine if the oil industry allowed us to learn from its environment experts as they faced the challenges of their industry, or the financial sector helped us to understand its complexity by letting us understand the "nerdiness" of its best minds. Imagine if we got good at passing on what we know to each other and took responsibility for each other's learning.

As with most things this isn't new. The idea of assistants or apprentices has been around for millennia and is still the most effective way of picking up knowledge and skills. When I was a sound engineer in radio we learned best from watching and working with more experienced operators than ourselves. We benefited from their thoughtful approach to their work and their desire to keep their skills alive by passing them on. But with the onward move of technology and the rising cost of people this apprenticeship process fell by the wayside. Suddenly people were meant to come out of sterile training programmes as fully fledged experienced operators. It didn't work.

We also learned at the cutting edge. When you had made a significant mistake on air the first thing you did was make your way to the bar, order a stiff drink, and regale anyone within earshot of the horrors you had just brought upon the listening public. The others around would stand nodding their heads muttering "ooh I'm not going to do that then" and informal learning took place.

In the absence of apprenticeships – or with reduced time for drinking – how else do you pick up this current, pertinent learning? Using social web tools of course!

The web is all about learning. Whether it is finding out what to see at the cinema or where your friends are at the moment, we take for granted that we use the web to help us learn things all day in all sorts of situations. We are sucking in more information than ever before from a wider range of sources and for a broader range of purposes. Learning by asking questions in online forums or by watching YouTube videos that explain in great detail the very thing we are trying to understand. When I need to understand how to use my latest camera, I look for the information on the web; when my Dad decides to learn the cello, he watches detailed videos on how to perfect his fingering technique on YouTube. This is learning on steroids.

Inside organizations much of the use of social tools in enterprises is focused on this day to day learning of how to do things better. Whether it is Mars Foods with their active networks of bloggers writing about food science and packaging technologies, or Japanese shipping firm NYK sharing detailed information about their fleet and the berths they use around the world on their wiki, businesses are discovering that being able to learn from each other is the best way to keep up with the latest information.

And if you are trying to keep up with the latest information, the answers you are looking for may well not be in books or manuals yet. They may only be in the heads of other people. The best way to get access to that knowledge is through online conversations with the people themselves. Sometimes you get direct access to the leaders in their fields. Many people have been blown away by being able to tweet or email a famous author of the book or article they are reading and get an immediate response! This is true in work too. Rather than trying to get on a course or read an out-of-date manual, being able to ask the question of the person who knows the answers you are looking for in real time is very powerful.

So the social web is all about learning, but currently much of this passes un-noticed by the formal business world. In fact part of the problem is that it is not accredited by anyone. A few years ago I worked with The Open University on a project called Social Learn which aspired to re-invent the university for the Internet age and two things seemed most important to me. Firstly that any institution helping me with my learning should come to me where I am learning rather than expecting me to go to a special, even virtual, place. And secondly I wanted them to come up with a method of recording and reflecting my learning in such a way that it could be accredited and allow me to gain the maximum advantage from it.

The same is true in a work context. The most current information about how to do things is in the heads of the leading proponents of the skill. It is not in the heads of trainers. If I want to keep my skills up to date and keep at the leading edge of my business I need to follow the people who know what they are talking about and are going faster than the rest. People don't always want to give up the time to attend formal training but are increasingly willing to learn from each other on an ongoing online basis. In the future we will have to find ways of recognizing and rewarding this kind of learning.

The last aspect of learning and social tools is very much about you as an individual. Many of us pass through our careers with little encouragement or inclination to stop and think about how and why we do what we do. In fact you often don't know what you know until you start to explain it to someone else or to write it down. "If you can't do it teach it" – in the process of teaching you will reinforce your learning. If you can't do it try to blog it. Thinking about what you do and why will enhance your learning and show up any gaps you might have. This is one of the least publicized benefits of having a blog.

Having a place to write and a reason to think about what you are doing and why, what is working or not, and taking that moment for reflection can have enormous benefits in terms of learning and, frankly, emotional well being. How many of us succumb to an overall feeling of unease or stress without really understanding why? Picking your challenges apart and writing them down helps to place them at a distance that allows you to see them for what they are. If we have the courage to do this in a way that is visible to other people then the potential for learning increases exponentially.

We are learning all the time – we always have been – but the Internet and social tools speed up the process. For the first time we can easily and cheaply share what we know with others whether in a blog post about a business insight or a YouTube video on how to fix a technical problem. We have at our disposal the collective wisdom of hundreds of thousands of people. Imagine what we will be capable of if we are all willing and able to use it!

Things to remember:

- People learn best from each other and access to the real experiences of real people is one of the most effective ways to learn.
- Social tools are one of the best ways of providing this access to real experience and much of the web is actually all about learning
- Formal education is struggling to keep up with these changes but having our online learning recognized and enhanced will increasingly matter at work.
- Even if no one else learns from what you write in social tools, you do – and this may be the greatest reward.

6

"WRITING OURSELVES INTO EXISTENCE"

Developing your own skills and knowledge has never been easier. In fact it has never been more in our own interests to build skills and capabilities as the world of work becomes more unpredictable. The web gives us access to all sorts of wonderful resources for learning but it does more than this. It helps us understand ourselves and the world around us in context. It helps us make sense of things. It helps us "be" more.

There is something about the process of blogging that makes you more self-aware. You become more thoughtful about yourself and your place in the world. In the reactions of others to your writing you get a different perspective, possibly for the first time, on how others see you. While this can be scary at first it can also be liberating. David Weinberger, one of the authors of *The Cluetrain Manifesto* – the classic book explaining the Internet and its impact on society – once described blogging as "writing ourselves into existence". This is very much how it feels. It is like being at university. Yes you were there to learn the formal stuff, but most of the benefit came from having the luxury of time to discover yourself before the world of work started to mould and shape you. Blogging gives you a little of that space back. Space to be yourself. Space to discover yourself. The ability to "try out" different aspects of yourself in relative safety.

Being able to see changes over time in what is effectively an online diary is fascinating and revealing. What was bothering you five years ago? Is it still bothering you? Have you moved on? Why not? Few of us maintain conventional journals these days and blogs may be our only experience of this sort of reflective writing. It is something you get better at. Both the writing and the reflection. You notice more, become more honest, get better at working out what you think about things around you. If you are a manager this can be the most powerful aspect of these tools. Even if no one else reads your blog, having the reason to sit down for even just fifteen minutes to think about what the day meant for both you and the people around you, can be very powerful. What worked, what didn't, what you would do again and what you wouldn't, what you want to pass on to others.

This sort of self-awareness and thoughtfulness is not just an indulgence. Its absence has had a profound effect on the way we run businesses and ultimately on the bottom line. Arguably much of the dysfunctional behaviour we see in large organizations is driven by the actions of people, mostly men it has to be said, who haven't been brought up to see the value in being self-aware. It has been seen as a sign of weakness to "think too much" so we have people – often scared, out of their depth, not sure of what they are doing – taking it out on others with their demanding and unreasonable behaviour. Much of this has been able to be kept hidden from general view. Rants in boardrooms or bullying managers become accepted as just the way things are or ignored.

Online this is harder to do. Once interactions start taking place in open virtual places, the whole world gets to observe and make judgements about your actions. It can be very revealing when someone who is used to throwing their weight around in "real life" starts to do so online. People's reactions become more apparent. Things you thought were acceptable may become more obviously not so. Working out these reactions and what they mean for the individual is often the first time people have been forced to face up to their impact on others. The process of thinking and writing about this can be revelatory to many people, especially senior managers.

Being open about your failings isn't everyone's cup of tea and wouldn't be acceptable in every workplace, but just a little more openness about your failings in front of your staff might just be the best way to improve your working relationships. Being seen not to know, and being willing to ask for help, can be the best way to make other people feel valued. It also signals to them that it is OK not to know everything all the time. This creates the sort of culture where people are more willing to open up and share what they know to everyone's mutual benefit.

Having been faced with this direct form of feedback, and assuming you have decided that you want to change, blogs are such a great way to learn more about being more effective, more productive, and – to be honest – happier. There are a profusion of productivity blogs and personal development blogs out there on the web ranging from the awful to the really helpful. You can pick up tips and tricks to increase your personal effectiveness and also discover valuable resources online that you can make use of.

Following the reading habits of people you admire and want to emulate is one of the best ways to manage your own self-improvement and the web is a wonderful way to tap into these resources. As you walk this path of learning and growing you will find other people willing to follow you. One of the best ways of developing trust and effective networks is the feeling that you are travelling on a shared path. In the past these paths were hidden – now they can be seen and followed by others. Being open about challenges, being seen to work on them, not hiding behind facades are incredibly powerful if you have the courage to do so.

As you do more of your learning "in public" your relationship with your boss changes. Instead of the dreaded annual review where he pretends to remember you and what you have been doing, you can now have an ongoing diary of your challenges and your responses to them which will have been available to him all year. I know a primary teacher who writes his pupils' annual parent reports on Google Docs and gives the parent ongoing access to the reports through the term as he writes them. Imagine doing the same thing with annual staff reports. I am not naïve. Many have the sort of relationship with their boss that would make all this just a pipe dream. But as more of the bosses of the world have more experience themselves of "writing themselves into existence" they are more likely to adopt this approach with those who work with them.

An appetite for self-development will have an impact on training. Much of training in organizations is still "bums on seats" classes or their online equivalent. If more people get actively involved in their own shared learning activities then the need for centralized training changes or indeed diminishes. Giving people the resources to learn themselves will matter more. This might be teaching them the writing skills to express themselves online. It might be helping them identify likely networks of people to learn alongside. It might be just setting them up with the right tools and resources to enhance their learning.

The whole web is at some level about informal learning and we now have the option of tapping into this and seeing the workplace as our greatest opportunity to learn both about ourselves and the world around us. We have such a wonderful chance to grow and to learn through the use of these tools – especially in the context of work. It is often at work that we face our greatest challenges – suffer our worst defeats and celebrate our proudest achievements. Doing this growing and learning, all the time, in writing and sharing it with others, takes self-awareness and understanding of our world to a whole new level. Scary though it is, the opportunity for personal learning and the increased satisfaction that affords us is too great for us not to take part.

Things to remember:

- There is something about blogging that encourages reflection and increased self-awareness. Getting good at it allows us to "write ourselves into existence"
- Self-reflection is not common in most business environments and the lack of it causes all sorts of dysfunctional behaviour to be accepted as the norm.
- Problematic behaviour is harder to hide online and more people will become more aware of their impact on others.
- Once you decide to change, the web offers up huge potential for self-directed learning.
- Being willing to learn in public is a sign of strength, and collective informal learning builds stronger and more effective businesses.

7

LITERACY RE-DISCOVERED

Are we becoming a new generation of writers? Since the days when the main form of communication between people was hand written letters, there has probably never been a time when so many of us communicated with each other through the written word. No matter how short form the medium.

When you have somewhere to write, even something as unassuming as a blog or as constrained as a tweet, you start to notice more about your life. What is it in this situation that is interesting enough to write about? What do I think about it? What do I want to say? What do I want people's reactions to be? Socrates thought that "The unexamined life is not worth living" and this has probably never been so true as we rush headlong through life at ever increasing speed.

So why are so many of us sharing our thoughts and ideas online? All of this heightened awareness adds value even if no one reads what you have written. I was never a great diary writer and bought a fresh hardback diary each New Year only to barely make it through January updating it. And yet here I am still blogging after ten years, having written enough words to fill dozens of books, and having been read by hundreds of thousands of people over the years. Why do I do it? I do it because without writing my blog I wouldn't be me. It has become a part of me. I think about writing for it all of the time. I think about my blog without thinking – if that makes sense. I am constantly observing the world around me with the view to possibly blogging, or nowadays tweeting, about it. I am at serious risk of thinking in 140 character "sound bites".

Self-reflection hasn't traditionally figured high in the job skills of those in business but why not? Why is it seen as a bad thing to be thoughtful about what we do? Why is it seen as so presumptive to want to share those thoughts? An older relative once said to me "Oh yes blogging – isn't that just people expressing their opinions?" Well . . . yes . . . and what is so wrong with that? How else does the world ever change except by people sharing their opinions? The "right" to share opinions has been the preserve of the few. We have professionalized communication and taken it away from the ordinary manager or member of staff. This has allowed a disproportionate degree of influence to rest in the hands of a privileged minority. The culture of an organization is much richer than this monoculture would make it appear but it has, until now, stayed relatively hidden in illiterate obscurity.

There is something literate and even literary about this process of writing ourselves into existence. The honing of observational skills combined with the challenge of finding just the right turn of phrase to convey meaning. And unlike books or business reports, blogs and Twitter have the constraints of a limited amount of text to play with. Yes people write long blog posts but I for one rarely read them. There seems to be an optimal three to four paragraph size for a blog post and writing within that discipline is a skill. People have been kind enough to say in the past that I am good at encapsulating sometimes complicated ideas into that relatively small space. It often takes more effort to write a small amount of text than a large essay, as observed by Mark Twain – "I didn't have time to write a short letter, so I wrote a long one instead." With Twitter this is even more true and the delight of writing a haiku-like 140 character tweet that can shift people's ideas is profound.

In contrast with the precision, and concision, of online literary forms, much business writing is turgid, unfocused, and uninspiring. I have seen so many reports written to a formula that had to contain certain sections just because the standard template had them. People rarely write business documents with their audience, or even effective communication, in mind. In fact much business writing isn't even read! We fill the space with the same old words and end up with lifeless prose consigned to be stored in some hidden server never to be seen again. In fact I believe, as David Weinberger wrote, that documents are dead. Not only does a conventional document start dying as soon as we publish it, in the sense that its currency reduces, but the document format itself is less and less the way we communicate with each other.

Wikipedia has given people an experience of malleable, shared writing. It is so clearly an ever changing aggregate of the insights and knowledge of the many people contributing to its pages. Blogging showed people how ideas from various sources could be threaded together to construct meaning. Twitter has shown that it is possible to convey an idea in less than 140 characters in a way that can change the world. We are playing with and learning to use whole new aspects of the written medium. And it is a connected medium. Once you have written your blog post or tweet, if you are lucky others will read it. If you have done a good job you will stimulate their thinking and they might then comment on your post or write their own, stimulated by yours.

We get approval and reinforcement from those who agree with us and challenge from those who don't. We build webs of meaning using these linked ideas and construct shared meaning in a way totally different from the heavy, disconnected documents of the past. What if we taught the skills of this new kind of proactive, shared, self-reflection in schools instead of teaching our children to build spreadsheets and construct tedious PowerPoint presentations? What if we began producing creative, engaging writing that was capable of inspiring us? Imagine how much more effective our business communications would be, and hence how much more successful our businesses would be, if we brought energy, imagination, and vigour to our writing. Imagine how much more fun a literate business could be than our current illiterate ones.

Things to remember:

- Having somewhere to write like a blog or Twitter makes you more aware of what is happening around you.
- We are communicating more to each other through the medium of writing than we have done for decades.
- Writing an effective blog post or tweet is a literary skill.
- Much business writing is badly done and ineffective.
- The metaphor of the document has become a liability in the era of blogs and Wikipedia.
- Improving our writing skills and seeing it as part of everyone's job will improve the effectiveness of our organizations.

8

MASS ILLITERACY

Despite the fact that much of the communication done in organizations is in writing, we are not generally very good at it. We don't take it seriously. We don't get taught how to do it. Blogging and other social tools are tools that encourage literacy of a new kind. This could revolutionize business.

We touched on how poor business communication is in the last chapter. Much of what we have to read at work is badly written, uninspiring, and written for all the wrong reasons. Social tools, in contrast, are like a new form of literature. Being literate in a new way. Writing in a way that calls on you to develop skills that have normally been the preserve of published writers. Firstly when you have a blog or tweet you have a reason to notice things. You become more observant. When you are out in the world, your skills of observation improve and you notice more – what is working, what isn't, why things happen the way they do. Having noticed these things you then try to work out the meaning of what you have observed. Why is it interesting, what is the essence of it, how would you convey this essence to others? Then you have to work out how to say all this in words. You have to get good with words, and with translating ideas into words that work. Over time you get better at this. Like every other form of writer – and I am not ashamed to use that word in this context – you refine your skills and, dare I say it, your art. Why be squeamish about the art of effective communication?

To be effective, communication has to work on a number of levels. Yes it has to convey information, but it also has to grab the reader and speak to them about something they care about. Arguably a lot of business communication fails because it misses out this last bit. No one cares. They don't care if you read it, and don't care if you understand it. When you write your own blog you do care. It is like wearing your heart on your sleeve. It is also a legacy. It is a snapshot of what you think, and why, that will persist. It is "written" not spoken. It is less ephemeral than conversation but more transient than conventional business documentation.

How do you balance your personal style, your voice, with the norms of business? Can you? Should you? Isn't the whole point of the changes we are seeing that we are stretching what is considered "business like"? Sometimes you will write cautiously, sometimes you will be brave. Sometimes you will write a lot, sometimes a single line will do. Many are discovering the haiku-like qualities of a tweet, the challenge of summing up an idea or conveying an impression in 140 characters. This calls on a discipline and concision sadly lacking in much of the turgid writing accepted as the norm in business. As we have seen in various global events, a well aimed tweet can change the world – why shouldn't it change your organization?

This is also a new kind of literacy. It is joined up literacy. What you write isn't considered in isolation. What you said last week and last year will still be visible online and you will have to take this into account. If you have changed your views on something people will be able to see that you have done so. Also, joined up literacy means building on the ideas of others and making that debt explicit. This was why Sir Tim Berners-Lee invented the web at CERN – to overcome the tendency to write as if no one had ever written about the topic before and to make explicit the connections between ideas and topics. There is a knack to hyperlinking well. Judging how many links to put in a blogpost or wiki page is a skill. Look at the depth of information offered by the vast number of links on the average Wikipedia page. When you link to other people's content you are conferring value on their writing. Some people only ever do link blogs which link to interesting content elsewhere with minimal comment as to why it is interesting. This is a lot of what goes on on Twitter. It is curation of ideas. A level up from this is short form blogging where the content might be original or build on the ideas of others. There is an art to writing in such a way as to develop connections and ongoing shared sense making. Effective blogging is like lobbing pebbles into a pond. You get better at lobbing bigger pebbles and making bigger ripples.

The shared sense making which all of these tools enable is very powerful. When you read and link to a group of people you get to know them at a profound level. You share insights and understanding and in your writing you develop together. I remember realizing, in the early days of blogging, that most of my group had been writing in a melancholy vein for a couple of days. It struck me that it was as if we were passing on mood with our connected writing. This connected thinking shapes not only what we understand but how we feel. This is even more obvious on forums where things can take a turn for the better or the worse with feelings and emotions rippling around the online space. I can think of many occasions when a positive mood has been consciously spread through thousands of people all deciding to cheer up in the face of a big challenge.

These forces are what you want to have in business – and what represents a risk. You want positive feelings about your product to amplify around the web and energy around your latest initiative to spread on your intranet. But equally you dread negativity spreading unchecked. This is where your efforts to steer things towards positive outcomes, and away from negative ones, are required to be literate. Finding the right tone of voice, or that perfect turn of phrase, can make all the difference between success and failure. Unlike the measured language of business documents, you have to grab the situation and make sure what you say gets the right response. Often you have to do so quickly and without the ability to refer to others or to edit. This is a new form of literacy and one that will cost you dear if you don't understand it. It is a bit like each of us having the opportunity, and responsibility, of rallying the troops or calming an angry crowd. And doing so in public. And having our every word recorded for posterity. We won't know when we write it if that sentence will be the one everyone will remember for years to come. We have to be bold, and we have to get it right.

Things to remember:

- Social tools call for a new form of literacy and you have to work at developing these skills.
- Communication has to not only pass on information but also to make people care about what is being conveyed.
- This new literacy can be more precise and effective than our current sanitized forms of business communication.
- Linking to other people's ideas enables joined up, disseminated, generation of ideas and collaborative learning.
- Improving your corporate culture and the collective mood of your organization will increasingly depend on your literary skill.

9

STATING THE OBVIOUS

Most of us are used to limiting what we say in writing, and even sometimes what we think, for fear of ridicule or criticism. None of us like having to deal with criticism and online it can be even more unrestrained. If you are going to have influence in our increasingly online world in the future, you need to build the courage to have a go and say what you think – even when there is the possibility that people will laugh at you and attack your ideas.

One of the scariest things about starting to say what you think in writing is the prospect of people disagreeing with you. Will they laugh? Will they think that what you are saying is trite and obvious? When I first started writing my own blog I did so anonymously. I called it "The Obvious?" because it was me overcoming my reticence about stating the obvious. The question mark is not a mistake. It is me shrugging my shoulders and suggesting a doubt in my mind rather than making a bold assertive statement.

We all learn to filter what we say from an early age in school. "What will earn the approval or disapproval of the schoolteacher?" "What will make my mates laugh at me?" This fear is even more true in the workplace. "What if my boss disapproves of my views or thinks I am talking nonsense?" "What if my peers snigger behind my back the next time they see me in the canteen?" These are not trivial concerns to overcome. We have largely learned that it is safer to keep our heads down at work. Not to rock the boat. To go with the flow if not the herd. Turning this around is a considerable personal challenge for most of us. Not only expressing what we think out loud for everyone to hear, but doing so in writing that will potentially be visible forever. It is easy to go numb in the face of this challenge. To dismiss our thoughts as trivial or wrong. "Who am I to think this?" "Who am I to say this?"

The trouble with this pre-filtering is that what you know never gets heard. We need to know what you are thinking and noticing, even if you don't think it is important. I know this is counter-intuitive, but the truth is that we need more stuff. Without more stuff you don't get good stuff. We need more people overcoming their reticence and stating the obvious, because otherwise too much will stay hidden and unsaid. You probably even keep things you know hidden from yourself. Until you start writing down your thoughts they have no power. Writing them down helps you clarify your thinking and doing so in public helps us all learn.

If what you are thinking is making you uncomfortable or embarrassed, even before you write it in public, think about why. Is it because you suspect you are wrong? Is it because you don't know enough? Is it because it is not your job to think these things or know these things? All of these are important questions for you to answer, at least for your ongoing effectiveness, if not your sanity. Think about them in writing. If possible think about them out loud. If you face issues about what you are thinking then almost certainly others will too.

Often when one person has had the courage to open up and express tentative ideas, or the beginnings of an insight, other people will respond with "I am so glad someone has said that – I have been thinking it for ages" or "I think that too, but didn't have the courage to say it out loud." These responses bolster your confidence about stating the obvious and make it easier next time. Maybe next time you will be braver and say more, think harder, and make more outrageous claims.

Get more interesting conversations going by tapping into what more people have been thinking but not saying. If you keep doing this and adding value to other people with your writing, you will be seen as someone who asks good questions. If your answers are good you will be seen as someone who knows what they are talking about. Very soon you will go from worrying about people laughing at you to finding that people come to you for advice and your boss is beginning to notice.

Beware those who laugh at you out loud. Ask yourself why they are laughing. There are very strong collusive forces at work in business and people tend to chop down the tall poppies. If they have become comfortable keeping their heads down, they won't like it when they see someone else standing up for what they think. Keeping things "business like" is often a cover for keeping people in their comfort zones. The very people who go on about the need for creativity and innovation are often those who resist the dissent and messiness inherent in both of those big words.

But maybe you are talking rubbish? If you are, then the problem is not that you are saying it, but that you are thinking it. You have to take responsibility for your own ideas and knowledge. If your ideas are wide of the mark – think harder. If you don't know what you are talking about – find out more. This is the evolutionary force of the web at work. It becomes more obvious who knows what they are talking about and who doesn't – and the risk of being one of the latter becomes apparent very quickly. Finding out that you don't know what you are talking about may be painful but it is better to do it sooner rather than later.

What if people disagree with you in your comments on your blog or on a forum? This can feel pretty bruising. I was going to say that it is painful at first but to be honest the bruising feeling doesn't go away. If you have put your heart and soul into a post and if the first commenter trashes it, it hurts. It is hard not to get defensive and overreact. It can feel like a direct challenge to your authority, especially if you are meant to be an expert. It is. But you need to be seen to be able to deal with it. How you deal with it can be more powerful than the original post. If you are seen to be big enough to accommodate alternative viewpoints or, even better, admit that you are wrong and are prepared to learn, then you come out of the exchange stronger. This fear of being contradicted gets worse the more expert you are or the more senior you are. You have more to lose. But then if you don't want to atrophy and rest on your laurels, you want to be challenged and, if you have any sense, you will seek these situations out.

The worst reaction in many ways to you saying what you think is to get no reaction. The time when you work hard on a blog post, research the ideas, lovingly craft the prose, and then press publish expecting the world to fall at your feet in gratitude – and nothing happens. Not a comment or a repost or a reference. Not a sausage. You can hear the virtual tumbleweed blowing through the Internet. If there doesn't appear to be any response it doesn't mean you haven't had an impact. Sometimes people have taken in what you said and digested it even if they didn't make it obvious at the time. I have often had posts that appeared to have been ignored only to have someone refer to them positively in conversation years later. And then there is the opposite. The time when you bang off a quick daft idea after too many glasses of red on a Saturday night and the whole world goes berserk and thinks you are a genius. Who said life was fair!

If we are going to make the most of our online, literate futures, we have to become more comfortable with standing up and being counted – with stating the obvious. It takes courage to do this but having that courage helps us to grow and understand ourselves better. We grow stronger as we face criticism and we develop our ideas as we take it on board. We learn to write for ourselves but to love it when others read what we have written. Doing this we grow stronger both as individuals and collectively.

Things to remember:

- It takes courage to share your thoughts in writing and in public.
- Get in the habit of capturing your thoughts in writing, even if you are the only person who ever reads them.
- Be brave about sharing your thoughts and ideas in public. Most people will be glad you did.
- If you are worried about what you don't know or what you think – do something about it.
- You won't always see a response to what you have written but this doesn't mean there hasn't been one.
- If we all learn to say what we think, we all get to grow stronger.

10

VOLUME CONTROL ON MOB RULE

Yes the Internet can amplify both the good and bad in mankind, but we forget that we all have a volume control. We get to choose what we pass on and amplify, what we push back against, and what we simply ignore.

We all have a volume control on mob rule. We don't have to link to people causing trouble on the web unless we feel they have a valid point. In fact once you have an online presence it is in your interests to only link to things that enhance your reputation rather than make you look stupid. Once you have a degree of credibility on the web you don't want to lose that credibility by wasting it on pointing to things that either aren't true, or are overly abusive or negative. But we have to be aware of this power and exercise it responsibly. We can turn the volume control on mob rule up or down and we have to think carefully about whichever we do – and its consequences. What are you linking to? What are you saying by linking? What are the likely consequences?

You don't of course have to link to things. There are ways that you can talk about things that you feel are negative without increasing their exposure on the web. We can refer to things but not link to them. I have often commented on something I disagreed with, or disapproved of, and not linked to it because I didn't want to increase its Google rankings. I am able to pass on condemnation without increasing their profile. Not only do we have the choice to not link to something if we don't want to increase its profile but we also all have the possibility of moderating its impact with our own writing and comment. If we see someone unfairly criticizing a product or service we should say so and make the opposite case. For a business, having your customers defend your product or service against an attack can be the most powerful form of marketing.

Many corporations fear mob rule. The prospect of a lone customer slagging them off on the Internet or worse, packs of angry bloggers rounding on them over some corporate slip up or dodgy product. It is true that if enough people say often enough on the web that your product or service is dodgy then you do have a problem – but that is just it. It takes enough people, taken seriously enough, by enough other people, for you to have a real problem. And if that is the case then your problem is probably real and you need to be dealing with it anyway!

There is something in all of us that is drawn to tales of disaster and misfortune. This is no different on the web. Brands are much more likely to hear complaints than compliments. There is also a voyeuristic aspect on the web that can be disconcerting and draws us to misfortune like rubbernecking car crashes on the motorway. Arguably we will never get away from this but we do have more control over it than before. We all have a responsibility to exercise this control. One of the reasons that I got into blogging in the first place was a strong feeling that my children would inhabit this virtual space even more than I have and if it is going to be habitable we have to make it habitable. It is like the wild west. If we leave it to the gunslingers and the pornographers it will stay uninhabitable. If we want to make it habitable we have to make it so by being in there behaving in productive and positive ways and showing that it can be a tool for good.

This is why I get so annoyed at the media tendency to sensationalize the seedy side of the web. I have appeared a couple of times on BBC Television to comment on children and the risks they may face on the web. On each occasion I have taken the broadcasters to task as I see them as part of the problem. It was them making the parents paranoid about the web that was putting the children at risk. The parents make assumptions about sites like Facebook based on what they are fed by the media. As a consequence they don't learn about the web, don't understand what is happening, and are less able to have the sensible conversations they need to have with their kids about what is safe, what is not, and how that translates to the web.

There is something ultimately democratic about our ability to fan the flames of a story or douse them with our comment. Like any form of democracy this entails responsibility. I remember many years ago in the early days of blogging a couple of famous bloggers got involved in a pretty unseemly online spat. I felt that this was sending a bad signal about how to behave online and, adopting my best judgemental west of Scotland online accent, I waded in and told them to behave. Now in retrospect this may not have been the most productive way of dealing with the situation, but I don't regret my inclination to take some degree of responsibility for what was happening.

This isn't like mainstream media. We have power to make immediate and effective responses to anything we see "not working" on the web and must take responsibility for exercising that power. This is what I believe the web gives us the best tool to achieve. Millions of us taking responsibility for what we choose to turn the volume control up or down on, and in doing so taking part in shaping the world of ideas in a way that has never been possible before.

Things to remember:

- We all have the power on the web to choose what we point to and what we don't. We need to exercise that power responsibly.
- We can also mitigate the effects of negativity on the web by standing up and saying what we think about what we see as bad behaviour.
- Human nature tends to focus on the negative and take the positives for granted.
- If your product or service is being criticized online and no one is leaping to your defence, then you probably have a problem!
- Unlike mainstream media we have a degree of control over what gets amplified through our network and what gets turned down.
- We each have to take responsibility for shaping our online environments and they will be what we make them.

11

DEALING WITH A BOSS WHO DOESN'T "GET IT"

Not everyone gets social media – to say the least – and this is likely to be the case for some time. There is a very strong chance that your boss is someone who doesn't understand the web or social tools. How do you deal with this?

We have all at some time faced the challenge of a boss who doesn't understand what we are doing. The need to "manage upwards" is not new. But what is new is that with social tools our bosses can see what we are thinking – in black and white – and this can be intimidating. However, if you are worried about your boss reading what you are saying on your blog, what are you actually worried about? Are you worried that he won't approve of you and your ideas? Are you worried that you will expose the fact that you know less than he thinks you do!? Isn't this a problem in real life anyway, not just in your blog? In fact blogs are rarely the issue in themselves but they do open up cans of worms and make us aware of things that were already issues and that, arguably, we should have been dealing with.

One of the fundamental outcomes of social media is people finding their own voice. Having the confidence to say what they think in public and standing up to disagreement or disapproval when they do so. This is as much about assertiveness and self-respect as it is about anything else. It is about your relationship to the world about you, the important people in your life – even your relationship with yourself. What do you feel comfortable talking about? What don't you feel comfortable talking about? Why?

Disapproval is a very strong force and for many of us one of the hardest to overcome. This is especially true if the disapproval is coming from the one who determines your salary! But if you are in a situation where you face constant disapproval you have two choices – accept any criticism as valid and do something to improve yourself, or decide that you are in a no win situation and get out. Either way, using social tools can help.

If you need to improve your skills, or increase your self-awareness, social tools can be an invaluable source of opportunities. Unlike other conventional forms of self-improvement, such as expensive training or attending conferences, reading blogs about your area of expertise is mostly free. Connecting with others in your field is also free and powerful. They give you not only the ability to learn from others but also to be able to share your own ideas and develop them. If you decide that you do need to get out of your current situation, making what you know more visible to others through social tools can be a great way of securing your next move. Even if your boss doesn't appreciate you, others in your networks will. Being seen to know what you are talking about to as wide a network as possible is the best way to sidestep an unappreciative boss.

What if you aren't encouraged to blog officially through work? There is nothing to stop you doing so from home. It is possible to build a reputation as someone who is knowledgeable and helpful in your area of expertise without the need for anyone to know where you work. Even if you have to blog anonymously, and you obviously need to act responsibly and be careful not to be indiscreet about concrete aspects of what you do, it is still possible to talk in general terms about the things you have expertise in. You can write about your profession or topics relevant to your work and build your reputation through sharing what you know. For instance, when I started blogging I blogged anonymously to begin with as it felt easier than trying to ask permission or to explain to my boss what I was doing. As I became better known and people knew it was me this became inappropriate, but it did get me started.

Often bosses are disapproving because they don't know better. In fact a lot of work I do with organizations is at the request of someone who "gets it" and who wants me to come in and influence their seniors. As a grey haired, former senior manager in a blue chip organization like the BBC, I get to have conversations with bosses that may be difficult if you work for them, but there is no reason you can't do this yourself. It is always possible to find some way to help your boss understand what is going on and what the benefits are.

Maybe your boss is nervous because he understands the potential of social media all too well. Once people learn that they can find each other, share their knowledge, and work together the roles of many managers will change if not disappear. This is frightening. However the good managers will make the effort to adapt and will continue to add value in the more networked world we are moving into. Many of them will be old enough to have children active on the web and see what is happening but they may not be comfortable talking to them about it. Or maybe they get the point of social tools outside work but can't see how to map them to the business context. Why not help them? Why not help your boss to understand the benefits to their business – and to them as individuals – of getting to grips with the social network world? Start the conversation rather than worrying in silence. There is a real danger that we assume that our boss knows everything. Often they don't and may be embarrassed about admitting this. Make it easy for them to do so.

Broaching the subject of your plans and hopes for social media is hard. You have to use words that your boss is unfamiliar with, and you have to justify this thing that no one is really that sure of yet, without really knowing what the results will be. It is too easy to fall into abstract concepts or to try to beat them to death with case studies from other organizations. What dawned on me eventually was that instead of asking for permission for something your bosses don't understand, ask for forgiveness for something that has worked. I realized that if the new world I was trying to help flourish was based on networks, and advocacy, and trial and error then that was what I should do. I got on much better when I stopped writing reports and going to so many meetings, kept myself out of the lime-light, and got on with doing things.

To achieve this I had a couple of senior people above me who minded my back and managed upwards while I got on with building platforms and encouraging their use. They weren't necessarily in my own direct chain of command but were influential in the business. They didn't always know what I was up to, or even understand what I was talking about, but they trusted me enough to let me get on with it. This was invaluable. You will probably have to be a bit tactical like this – and also a bit political with a small "p". If you can't get support from your boss, see if you can get support from their peers. Without actually going behind their back, make sure that enough people who talk to your boss know what you are doing and see the benefit in it. If he or she hears good things about you at enough meetings from people they respect then the approval will eventually rub off on you. Try to find this kind of support and cultivate it. Find senior people who get what you are trying to do and enlist their support. Don't make enemies of them or scare them. Keep talking to them in their language about what you are doing and why – even if they occasionally glaze over!

The final thing to say about dealing with your boss is that social media is not, as some would make out, a bottom up revolution. We are not talking worker solidarity here! These tools, and what they offer, are as attractive to those in the middle and the top of your organization as they are to those at the bottom. Being understood and having influence is attractive to everyone no matter what their position. And indeed everyone has a different per-spective and something unique to offer. In this spirit, offer social media as an opportunity rather than a threat to your boss. Show them blogs written by other managers in your business. Show them some of the high profile blogs written by executives on the web. Explain to them, gently, that there is more chance of them being listened to through an interesting and well written blog than there is sending long tedious memos. Get them interested, help them understand, and have fun getting them as excited about this changing world as you are.

Things to remember:

- We may fear disapproval from our boss when we start to write but it is the underlying issues we may have to deal with.
- If you reveal problems of competence or trust, seize the opportunity and face these head on.
- If you can't use social tools inside work, develop your experience and personal brand outside.
- Be responsible in your use of external platforms but seek to build your skills and networks.
- Enlist senior support from wherever you can – even if they are not your direct manager.
- If your boss doesn't understand social media – help them to.
- Social media is not a bottom up revolution. They can be useful to people at all levels. Having a voice and being heard is a universal human need.

12

THE MORE YOU GIVE
THE MORE YOU GET

The days when you could get away with not being noticed at work are passing. Being seen, and being seen to know what you are talking about, are becoming more important. This will be a wrench for some and a liberation for others. It has never been easier, or more fun, to share what we know. Being willing to share and help others is becoming an important factor in successful business.

For a significant number of people a survival tactic at work has been keeping their head down. Doing what is asked of them, and no doubt doing it well, but not rocking the boat by questioning things or suggesting that things could be done better. It has been possible to get through an entire career on this basis. Well . . . it used to be. It is increasingly unlikely that anyone will manage to do so in the future as more people spend more time learning and sharing in online environments. Not being seen, and not being seen to know what you know, will carry a higher price.

It is increasingly important to be seen to add value. To be seen to be knowledgeable and willing to share your knowledge. In the old days "knowledge is power" used to mean holding on to it and only giving it out judiciously to certain people. In an Internet world there is no point in having knowledge if people don't know you have it, and if you are not prepared to share it. Web tools enable more knowledge to flow more readily around your organization. Taking part in this process is going to be more obviously a part of being productive than ever before. Being able and willing to share your knowledge will become a key business skill.

So, if keeping yourself to yourself isn't as safe as it used to be, what should you do instead? The best way to make yourself indispensable is to know really useful stuff, be seen to know it, and be willing to share it. This is what blogging and other social tools enable you to do more effectively than ever before. Keeping a blog about what you do, and why, makes you more aware of all aspects of your job. If you write well and people find value in what you know, your profile starts to increase. If enough people find what you are writing of interest and value then your credibility and status really start to improve. I have seen examples where people in remote parts of organizations, holding jobs without real power or influence, started to offer thoughtful, helpful answers to questions on an internal forum such that their power started to increase significantly. In contrast there were people in big offices with fancy job titles who, even if they did know a lot, we never got to find that out. They were obviously not willing to share what they knew with others.

The benefits of improving your profile aren't limited to your own organization either. Being willing to share what you know with networks of industry peers is a very powerful way of increasing your profile. Niche, specialist jobs, especially, may only have a small number of people who have that specific knowledge and being able to share this knowledge on the web will really increase your own and your organization's credibility. Obviously you need to be sensitive about what you share, but a lot of this sharing already happens at conferences and other networking events. Doing it online maximizes the benefit both for yourself and your organization.

In fact I talked a while back with a major oil company about the possibility of allowing their environment experts to connect with environment experts on the web, even those who were possibly antagonistic towards their company, as a way of building relationships and increasing their individual and collective credibility. Being seen as a good guy who wants to help has all sorts of personal and often immediate benefits. Reciprocity is a strong force on the web and being seen to be willing to help others increases the chances of them being willing to help you.

But, I hear you cry, what if I give away all of my knowledge? Well, for one thing, knowledge is one of the few things that doesn't diminish with use. I don't know any less by sharing what I know with you. I recently pulled together a comprehensive proposal for a potential client in which I shared a lot of knowledge and ideas. My wife was worried that I had given away too much, but I knew that, hopefully, being seen to know a lot, and being willing to share it, was my best chance of securing the contract. You could argue that writing all this stuff in this book is giving away my knowledge, but I know that being seen to know what I know hopefully increases my chances of picking up consultancy or speaking work. Writing this book is helping to reinforce my knowledge and build it rather than diminishing it.

If you can cultivate an environment where everyone feels more comfortable with sharing their knowledge then the risks diminish and the benefits accrue. But this isn't to say there isn't a competitive aspect to sharing your knowledge. Getting your ideas expressed first, and better, becomes important. Others may know what you know but if you write the best, most easily understood, blog post that becomes the most popular source of valued information then you have grabbed the high ground and will keep it until the knowledge or information changes or improves. You also attract a smarter bunch of people to your network. This increases your leverage. This is where quality matters more than quantity. Being really open, with useful stuff, and being respected by smart people is what it is all about.

Things to remember:

- Keeping your head down and not sharing what you know isn't as safe an option as it used to be.
- Sharing what you know is the fastest way to gain influence.
- Sharing what you know doesn't diminish its worth but instead increases its value.
- Being seen to know, and willing to share, important things first with an increasingly smart and influential network is the way to become successful in an online world.

13

"OOH, THAT'S INTERESTING"

Social tools are made up of networks of individuals taking an interest in what is happening around them. Finding patterns in what they have each found interesting enough to take the time to sit down and write about. It is the first time we have been able to experience the phenomenon of a collective "ooh that's interesting".

Let's start small. Let's start with you and your blog. When you have a blog you notice more. You find yourself thinking "Oooh that is interesting – I might write about that." When you are out and about doing your job or living your life you start to think about what things might be worth writing about and why. Why might I want to write about this thing I have just done or interesting event I have just seen? What would I say about it? What would people's reactions be when I write about it? What do I want their reactions to be? You start to be much more perceptive and thoughtful about what is happening to you and around you.

What is interesting enough to expend the effort required to sit down and write a blog post for fifteen minutes? What grabbed your attention enough? What was interesting enough that you didn't want to forget it? Is what you have just found interesting significant? Does it merit changing your mind about something or modifying the way you do things? If it is then you will want to write about it and say why it was so interesting.

So you store up all these thoughts and ideas and, when you are ready, sit down to write that blog post. If you have done a good job of writing it, other people will then go "Oooh that's interesting" and they might write about your idea or observation on their own blog, or comment on yours, or "Like" it on Facebook. All of this adds up to what I call "the collective ooh that's interesting process". This process helps us to filter the sea of information around us and adds layers of context to the meaning of the information. Networks of people noticing, commenting on, and sharing what they find interesting enough to take the time to write a blog post or a tweet about. In doing all of this noticing we work out together what is noteworthy and why.

We learn to follow people who are good at noticing interesting stuff – and tune out those who aren't. Each of us filters the world through our own eyes and those of others whom we trust and in doing so, by using online tools, we can vastly improve our experience of signal to noise. Even if what we are noticing is the output of conventional mainstream media we are still doing this collective filtering. Who is recommending which films or books? Do I trust their taste and judgement? Which news stories are being given credibility by people I trust? Which work policies are read and applied by my smartest colleagues? This collective noticing is what is behind viral videos on YouTube or mass campaigns on Facebook. It is shaping what we choose to give our attention to in whatever circumstances we find ourselves. For the first time what we are giving our attention to is visible to others as we do it.

This "ooh that's interesting" effect is even more powerful in the context of work. There is so much information generated in the modern corporation – some of it useful, some of it useless, and most of it in between. The trouble is that we have very few ways of deciding what is useful to us and what is not. Formal taxonomies and structured intranets are two ways of dealing with this challenge but they tend to reflect the perspective of a small subset of the organization and that may not be yours.

We have all experienced the frustration of looking for a piece of information that seems essential to us but wasn't deemed important by the person managing the database or the intranet site. What we want is access to what other people in circumstances similar to our own have found interesting or helpful. Of the sea of information available to you in your organization's stored data, what matters now in the circumstances you find yourself in and what did people in similar circumstances find useful? Once you have established internal forums or blogging networks you grow the ability to find the good stuff. You effectively create your own information systems through the networks you take part in and the people you follow. This means getting to the really relevant good stuff faster and more of the time.

So what is interesting and why? Is it the extreme and the unusual, or is it the ordinary and understated? Bloggers have different perspectives on what attracts their attention and you learn which type of blogger suits your own situation, temperament, and interests. Also your preferred way of digesting information matters. Are you more attracted to long, thoughtful posts or short, pithy sound bites? Blogs can range from link blogs, where people share links to interesting content with sometimes minimal additional content, to mini essays on complex topics. Do you prefer the short exchanges of Twitter or the conversations of LinkedIn? You will learn which approaches deliver the best value to you, on which topics, and in which circumstances. This takes an upfront investment of time and effort to build the necessary networks but the dividends are huge.

What you are building with these networks and tools are like information fishing nets that let you find the useful stuff and throw away the rubbish. The better and bigger your net the more likely you are to catch the right fish. To continue the analogy, nets need repairing. You need to maintain your network of bloggers to make sure that you continue to get the best signal to noise. You need to be sure that what they are noticing is relevant to you and not distracting you unnecessarily. If people are starting to add more noise than signal, remove them from your feeds. Beware of echo chambers, the tendency to follow people who agree with you. You have to take responsibility for stretching your learning and expanding your horizons. Go "off piste" occasionally and see what people who are not like you are finding interesting. See what people who disagree with you are thinking. Expand your idea gene pool all of the time.

Who follows you back is also important in this world of networks. Who follows you matters more than how many. It is possible to have a small number of influential and thoughtful people following you and have more influence than someone with tens of thousands of followers. Quality and not quantity is key when it comes to "ooh that's interesting" and you manage both your own output, and the people you follow, with this in mind. If you are going to add value to others and encourage them to follow you then you have to get good at noticing interesting stuff. You will have to add more signal than noise. You also have to be sure that you don't add noise to your own signal. When using Twitter be careful to get the right mix of useful links, your own insights, and the odd bit of info about where you are and what you are doing. There is nothing wrong with letting people know you are up and having a coffee. It is the online equivalent of walking into an office and saying good morning. But if that is all you say all day people are going to get bored!

Being awake and curious matters. Curiosity is a key skill. Not being so focused on "the way we do things around here" that you are blind to the unobtrusive but world-changing small detail. Wondering why things are the way they are and being good at musing on these topics is the way to attract followers. Much has been written about the attention economy, and where attention is limited how you use and spend yours matters. You have to be interested in what is happening around you and take responsibility for making the best use of what is available to you. Getting good at noticing things, refining your "oooh that's interesting" instincts – these are going to become key business skills as the world gets more complicated and making sense of it takes more effort. Our effort. Together.

Things to remember:

- Social networks are made up of individuals noticing things and sharing what they have found interesting.
- Having your own blog or Twitter account gives you a reason to notice more about the world around you.
- The collective process of "oooh that's interesting" helps us to find the useful and valuable information in the sea of information around us.
- This process helps us to improve the signal to noise in the system.
- Who follows you matters as much as who you follow and you have to be sure you add more signal than noise to your followers.
- Being curious is a key skill to develop to prepare us for the future.

14

THE NETWORK
OF NETWORKS

The power of the Internet is in the networks of people it enables. The connections and the relationships it fosters are what will change our view of how the world works.

It is funny how the word networking still carries negative connotations for many people. Hints of nepotism and "brown nosing". Trying to cheat your way into an inner circle by getting to know the right people. But in fact networks have always been the way to really get things done. Everyone builds up groups of people they trust, who in turn know other people they trust. We remember who knows who, where they work, and what they can help us with. This is how we get things to happen. If we were limited to doing things exclusively through the formal, command and control, hierarchies in our organizations then very little would get done. The real work gets carried out by networks of people who know and trust each other.

I had the advantage at the BBC of having worked there for a very long time and in a variety of very different roles. As a result I had built up a huge network of people in all sorts of places and was good at remembering who I knew, where, what they were good at, and what they might know that could help me. This meant that whenever I was faced with a problem I either knew someone who could help me or knew someone who knew someone who could. In fact one of my early jobs was as duty manager at the BBC World Service. This was the sort of role that was expected to deal with anything that didn't fit into the normal day to day. Bomb threats, Foreign Office messages, technical failures, natural disasters – we had to deal with it all and usually in a hurry. To do this you spent a lot of time building networks of people who you knew you could call on when you needed them. You did this by spending time with them, getting to know them, and going out of your way to help them if you could. This meant that when the shit hit the fan you had people you could call on to help.

In a later job setting up BBC DigiLab I was again paid to network. We ran a small unit dedicated to discovering new and interesting technologies that might make broadcasting better or more efficient. We then spread the word about those technologies around the business. In order to do so we started finding out who was interested in the new and the innovative. By the very new nature of this shared interest these people were few and far between so just the process of identifying them was useful. We then began to invite them to technology demonstrations and realized that a lot of the value to them was being able to meet others who shared their interest in new technologies. We then realized that there was an inherent value in these networks so we started organizing events that were designed to help identify and bring together dispersed groups with shared interests. It then struck us that the social tools appearing on the web were made for this stuff and we started to deploy them. Making these sorts of networks visible to others who hadn't had the opportunities I'd had was one of my main motivations in putting in the tools. They helped to make the informal networks visible for the very first time and made it easier to navigate them.

So why invest time and effort in building these networks? Because, at a very practical level, it makes life easier. Reciprocity is also an important aspect of building networks. Crudely stated it is "you scratch my back and I'll scratch yours". More benignly it is "the more you give out the more you get back". Building networks, online or off, also relies on being curious. Being interested in other people and what they know. Being willing to engage with them to discover what they know. There is a kind of mind set that finds networking useful and is good at it. It tends to appeal to people who are open to others and to new ideas. It doesn't tend to appeal to those who resist change and want to keep the number of their contacts small and limited. In fact I suspect that this open/closed distinction is a more useful one to explore when discussing the impact of social business than age or whether people are digital natives or not.

Maybe this actual example that happened to me recently will help clarify the power of building networks. I was booked to do a webinar with a university in the US. I was sitting in my office at home using my laptop and the students were sitting waiting to see me speak on a screen in a reasonably large lecture room somewhere on the east coast. I hadn't used the software they were using for the webinar before and when I came to try to use it the software wasn't connecting with the camera on my laptop. I tried changing every setting I knew of, and even tried reading the help files and raising the help desk. The help files were useless, as is so often the case, and the help desk was unmanned. So there I was about to face, in two minutes' time, a room full of a couple of hundred people being confronted with a blank screen.

But then I thought of Twitter. Out of the 5000 or so people who followed me at the time on Twitter someone was bound to know what I needed to do to get the system working. So I asked the question about how to get the camera connecting with the software and within seconds I had three answers. I then changed some settings, the camera worked, and moments later I was successfully talking to my audience. Now I can't think of another way I could have done that without Twitter. And the reason I could do it was because 5000 people were in my network. It also worked because they were prepared to help me because I had helped them in the past or they had seen me helping others.

Extrapolate this principle across the daily work of your whole organization and you can begin to see that building networks is one the most effective ways to increase the efficiency of whatever you do. Once you start to see the world in terms of these extended networks it changes how you view its structures and how you operate in them. You see rigid hierarchies intertwined with much more organic networks of individuals who have some sort of relationship with each other. You begin to cultivate these relationships and connect with people who extend your network and your ability to get things done. Building networks takes work. It also entails making an effort to maintain them. Make lists of people you'd like to get to know. Always look for opportunities to extend your network. Set yourself reminders to contact people. Make efforts to keep feeding the network with new people. Thank others who grow your network by introducing you to other people. Tend and care for your networks and they will take care of you.

Things to remember:

- Networks have always existed and are not new to the web.
- Networks intertwine our more formal structures and help us to navigate the people in our organizations.
- Building networks of people who are willing to help you is an important part of getting things done.
- Reciprocity is a strong force. Help other people willingly whenever you can and they are much more likely to help you.
- Investment in maintaining your network will pay you back tenfold and in real day-to-day practical ways.

15

REAL LEADERS HAVE FOLLOWERS

The concept of "followers" is now a familiar part of the social online world. This will soon be true at work too, where your ability to get things done will be down to the size and strength of your networks.

"The good news is you have 200 people working for you. The bad news is they don't see it that way." In that old joke lies a seed of truth about social media. We are all afraid that no one will follow us. How can you be a leader if you have no followers? How can you be a manager if no one hears what you say – how can you be an Internet guru if no one cares what you say – or buys your book? This is possibly the biggest hill to climb when it comes to social media, whether it is the lone manager opening up in writing for the first time, or a large corporation deciding to have a Facebook page. What if no one comes? What if no one finds us interesting or attractive?

Part of the problem is that in the online world your failure is quantifiable. We can all see how many fans your Facebook page has and how many flock to your competition. Anyone who cares to look can see that the numbers reading my blog are minuscule compared to the likes of Robert Scoble or Seth Godin. But does that stop me? Does that mean that my blog has no value? No. In fact you wouldn't have read this far in this book if what I said had absolutely no value. Wiley wouldn't have published it and you wouldn't have bought it if someone, somewhere hadn't found me interesting enough to pay me some attention. Any attention. Any attention is better than no attention. Some influence is better than no influence.

The numbers can be deceptive. I realize this may be just me rationalizing the fact that I don't have millions of followers, but it doesn't appear to matter because I count some very smart and influential people amongst my followers. As a result of my blog I have got to meet two of "the fathers of the Internet", the inventor of the worldwide web, and one of the founders of Google. The amount of leverage – certainly in the world I aspire to influence – that my readers have, is worth much more to me than having tens of thousands of followers over whom I have minimal influence and who themselves have minimal influence over others.

In this connected online world you maintain a following by being interesting and giving people something they need. Whether this is information or entertainment – or hopefully both – you have to give followers a reason to continue to follow you. You also have to treat them well and fairly. If you start to give them things they don't want, or treat them rudely or even with disdain, they will soon start to leave. In fact this is as true of the behemoths of the online world as it is true for you, since they too are subject to the fickleness of their users. Look at the rapid demise of MySpace. Not only can those with popular Facebook pages lose followers overnight – so can Facebook itself. If they abuse too many privileges, act in a cavalier way with their users – or indeed get complacent and start to add less value than a competitor – then they too will lose followers in a flash. The rapid growth of Google Plus has yet again shown the volatility of this online world and if you aren't adding value you get eclipsed bewilderingly quickly.

With followers comes responsibility. Individuals with significant numbers of followers can have the clout usually associated with elected politicians. We will have to learn how to deal with this. As I have said elsewhere in this book, we all have a volume control on mob rule, and those with larger numbers of followers who are prepared to be influenced by them, have larger volume controls.

In fact the word "followers" is probably wrong, as each of us will lead and follow in turn. We will become part of an ecology of others doing the same thing. Our impact on the ecology around us increases as we have more influence and so therefore does our responsibility. This can begin to feel onerous. We can go from worrying about what we say because we might look foolish to worrying about what we say because people might take us seriously! We would have the potential to abuse followers and mislead them. What we don't want for our own sakes are blind followers. We are all someone else's follower in some way. That balance between leader and follower is going to affect us all. We need to adopt both roles – and in fact often at the same time. Who am I allowing to have influence over me? Who am I hoping to influence in turn?

Imagine this fluidity in the context of work. Imagine if your influence was down to how much your work was useful to others rather than what your budget or job title was. I used to fantasize about our wiki – trust me – it sounds weird but I did. We watched it being used by large numbers of people daily to muster resources and run projects. I began to muse about what would happen if you ran all projects through the wiki and those projects that didn't attract enough interest, people, and resource, didn't happen. What would happen to all of those projects that get committed to just because someone senior has the authority and the budget – but which everyone thinks from the outset are daft? What if the only projects that happened were the ones that got enough followers? And having got started, and attracted enough initial followers, you would have to keep those followers. You would have to continue to add value to them and hold their attention. If your project started to turn into something else or lose relevance you would visibly lose support. How many over budget, late projects could we kill early with this approach?

Our assumptions about authority are changing. The nature of leadership is changing and you can't assume that your job title will give you the authority you need. Simply being higher up the food chain won't be enough. Effectiveness at work is becoming a PR exercise where you have to make an effort to convince people to do what you want them to do. Your influence and power will be down to the number of people you have helped and who are willing to help you. But hasn't it always been this way? Isn't this a more accurate reflection of the reality of work than the fiction of command and control? Real leaders have followers, and attracting followers calls for courage, consistency, and adding real value.

Things to remember:

- Leaders need followers and on the Internet we can all aspire to gain followers.
- The more followers you have, and the more influential they are, the more influence you will have.
- With influence comes responsibility. We all need to exercise our influence thoughtfully.
- At work your ability to get things done will increasingly be down to your ability to convince others to engage with your project.
- What costs could be avoided if only projects that got sufficient support came to fruition?

16

REAL FRIENDS

The word "friend" is widely used in online tools but what does it mean and does it matter?

People often sneer at the use of the word "friend" in online networking tools and ask how it is possible for anyone to have 5000 "real friends". I remember when the use of the word friend first became an issue. I think it was in the early days of Flickr, the photo sharing site. You could decide who could see which of your photos and they drew a distinction between contacts, family, and friends. One of my friends, real friends that is, took exception to this use of the word "friend" and refused to use it. I decided to follow his example and set all of my photos available to all of my contacts. This worked for a while but as I loaded more photos it became clear that there was a group of photos that I wanted to make available to a smaller group of people who were closer to me than the other contacts. These weren't family, the only other choice of contact category, so I gave in and started using the classification "friend" for this group of people. It didn't mean anything – but it started to stick.

The use of the word is still problematic even though now much more commonplace. Even in real life I struggle with what to call people I only know through the Internet. I pull myself up often when I use the word "mate" to describe someone I know through social tools. I tend to keep it for people I have met more than once and who I maintain a friendly connection with through the Internet but I am aware that the word may imply more to the person I am speaking to than it does to me.

As our networks have grown, the types of connections we have are changing. I still balk at allowing connection with people I have never met in LinkedIn and Facebook because doing so implies some sort of relationship while in many cases I don't know them, even online. I do connect with people I don't know sometimes though because I want to allow them to connect with me. It makes business sense to do so because they are presumably positively disposed towards me and allowing them to be "my friend" may lead to opportunities. However, particularly on Linke-dIn, the fact that the system uses inappropriate language and classifications to describe our relationship still rankles. The new social platform Google Plus introduces the idea of circles of connections which you can label yourself. This allows a finer grained distinction between different levels of relationship which is more in the user's control. It will be interesting to see how we adapt to this.

Even if we can learn to cope with the "friends" bit, the other half of "real friends" is problematic too. What does "real" mean? Does it mean you have to have met face to face? Is knowing someone face to face all it's cracked up to be? There are people I have worked with for years, working in the same office every day, who I barely know. Some would argue it is possible to be married to someone and not really know them! And yet there are many people I consider to be real friends on the Internet who I have never met in real life. Recently I got to meet a blogger I have been friends with for ten years. And I mean friends. Over the ten years we have got to read each other's thoughts on a whole range of topics and have experienced each other in more thoughtful ways than many people in more normal circumstances.

Good bloggers tend to open up and write thoughtfully about things that matter to them in a way that people don't tend to march up to you in real life and start philosophizing. As a result I know bloggers I have never met better than people I live next door to in my small village. The result of this is some very real friendships – however you choose to define that word.

Once you have built up these friendships online the result is that when you do meet face to face it is remark-able. The blogger I got to meet recently lives a very different life to me and we have very different views on some of life's most important subjects. I was a little nervous as I made my way to the restaurant where we had agreed to meet, because even though I had met many bloggers before and almost never been surprised or disappointed, there were no guarantees we would get on well. I needn't have worried. As soon as we saw each other there were broad smiles of recognition and we gave each other big hugs. We must have looked like long time friends to the people in the restaurant, and if we had told them that we had never met in a conventional sense they would have thought we were mad. Having got our initial greetings out of the way we immediately launched into an intense conversation about life, the universe, and everything, touching on topics that even people who know each other really well would normally steer clear of. We had the most wonderful evening, and to suggest that this is not real friendship is absurd.

Another measure of real friendship might be the willingness to help each other. Way back in the early days of blogging, when it was a much smaller world, I read a wonderful blog called "wood s lot" by Canadian Mark Wood. Mark still does a remarkable job of curating fascinating content from quality sources around the web and I got a lot of value from his ability to spot interesting content. Mark didn't blog much about himself but one day he announced that he was going to have to stop blogging because he wasn't going to have access to a computer. This was a real blow as I loved reading his blog and I found myself wondering why he wasn't going to have access. Was he going in to hospital? Was he running out of money? Was he about to be arrested?? I realized that I didn't care what the reasons were – I just wanted him to be able to keep blogging. So I decided to set up a PayPal account and encourage people to donate money to enable Mark to buy a computer. I blogged about this and by the end of the day we had several hundred dollars in the account. I arranged for this to be transferred to Mark and he kept blogging. I never really did find out the circumstances, and I never knew for sure that the money was spent on the computer. All I know is that he kept blogging. So was this friendship? I don't know – maybe it's something different. But it is not nothing.

This potential for a deep sense of connectedness that is different in so many ways from our conventional notions of friendship is one of the most exciting aspects of the Internet. The ability to form relationships unconstrained by geography, appearance, or nationality is new and exciting. These are real relationships and real friendships. In some ways more real and powerful than anything we have experienced before. We will use the Internet to create whole new networks of these powerful relationships and who knows, with this new found ability to be friendly towards each other, maybe we will find it harder to start wars?

Things to remember:

■ The use of the word "friend" online is problematic but we have got used to it.

■ You need to be thoughtful about who you connect with and why – whatever the language you use.

■ Online relationships can be just as powerful as those in the real world and we can sometimes know virtual friends better than real ones,

■ The Internet gives us new potential to meet our very human need to connect.

■ Our new opportunities for connectedness will change how we see the world.

17

TOO MUCH
OF A GOOD THING

Everyone agrees that having friends is a good thing but can you have too many friends? There is a lot of debate on the use of the word "friend" in online circles. What constitutes a friend? How can anyone have 10,000 friends? What are the limits of our online relationships?

B ritish anthropologist Robin Dunbar once proposed that there is an upper limit of 150 to the number of people with which each of us can sustain a meaningful social relationship. This has come to be known as the Dunbar number and is often bandied around in debates about online relationships as if it were an incontrovertible truth that those spending too much time with too many people were losers with no "real" friends.

Now this rather depends on two things – what we mean by the word "know" and the ways in which we maintain the connection. I reckon that, in the past, Dunbar was probably right and the maximum number of people I could sustain any sort of relationship with would be 150 – but online it is different. I know thousands of people online and I am often surprised at the depth of that knowledge. As an example, I keep a contact database of people that I know, both online and offline, on my computer. While going through the lists I am often struck by the number of people who, when I see their name, I can recall in terms of what they look like, where I met them, and what our relationship is. I reckon it is more than a thousand people that I am pretty familiar with and can remember significant details about without prompting other than seeing their names.

Online these numbers get even bigger. I "know" thousands of people in LinkedIn, Facebook, and Twitter. The total is probably about 7000 people I have at least a passing acquaintance with. OK so I get more prompting in terms of where I know them from and aspects of their lives that the tools help me with, but I still have a degree of recollection that would make it untrue to say that I didn't know them. On an ongoing basis I will have regular contact with at least half of them and will only occasionally have to check up who it is I am talking to and why.

And yet the number of people I know in the "real" world is still relatively small. Is my brain becoming wired to cope with larger numbers of people at a more superficial level with artificial aids? Does this matter? Is the nature of our relationships changing? There are plenty of people I know well in the conventional sense, who are of little use to me and who I might not even like. At the same time there are hundreds online who I have never shared the same space with but who I like and who help me on a regular basis. In many ways the larger, and perhaps more importantly the more diverse, the number of people I know, the more of a resource it is to me.

In the context of work, the larger the number of people you know, and who are positively inclined towards you, the more benefit you will accrue. A senior manager who blogged regularly in his business attracted a regular readership of thousands in his organization. His actual department totalled only around 1500 but eventually around 5000 were reading his blog on a regular basis. He was good at blogging and wrote about an interesting mix of the strategic and the personal, the large and the small. He combined this with a personal style and enough confidence to reveal his personality through his writing. This allowed many, many more people to "know" him in a way that simply wasn't true of the other senior managers who were just another name on the organization chart. This gave him increased influence and ultimately power. He also gained practical benefit. I remember him telling me that if he wrote on his blog about a particular challenge he was facing he would have people he didn't know coming up to him in corridors to offer help, advice, or information to help solve his problem.

I believe there is something fundamentally different and new about these networks and relationships. Yes, professional communicators have always had access to mass audiences but the connections are very superficial. There is a one-way communication most of the time and if it is two-way it is not on a personal level. This could not even be called a relationship let alone described as knowing each other. So we have an interesting situation where each of us as an individual is able to sustain larger and more effective networks than those with official responsibility for communications in our organizations. This combination of the size and depth of our potential networks gives us power. Manuel Castells writes about this in his excellent book *Communication Power* which explores this shift in the nature of our means of communication from broadcast to networked, and the increased power of the individual in this process.

Of course not all people in your network are equal. Some of them will themselves be more connected than others and some will be more willing than others to pass on to you the power of their own networks. By "choosing" the right people and making the effort to maintain connection with them you can generate and sustain significant networks of personal influence. You do this by many means but the most significant of these is reciprocity. Helping others is the best way of ensuring that they are willing to help you. You don't always know the people you are helping. You can help people by being willing to share what you know with them. You don't always know how, where, or even who will repay your efforts, but you do so in the confidence that people's willingness to help you will be down to how much you are seen as being willing and able to help others.

Does this constitute knowing people? Are these people your "friends"? Does it matter what we call them if we are able to extend the numbers of people who are positively disposed towards us beyond anything previously possible? Maybe we need new words. Maybe we are building new kinds of relationships. Maybe Dunbar was right but maybe it was for an old world that many of us are leaving behind.

Things to remember:

- The Dunbar number refers to the limit of 150 people that we can sustain a meaningful relationship with.
- Online tools allow us to extend the number of people we can maintain a meaningful connection with.
- Building networks that are large and diverse gives us more power – especially at work.
- Having extended networks of real relationships sometimes gives us as individuals more power and influence than professional communicators.
- Not all people we connect with are equal and we need a new vocabulary for the relationships we are able to build and sustain online.

18

GLOBALLY DISTRIBUTED CONVERSATIONS

The Internet is about "Globally distributed, near instant, person to person conversations."[1] Transcending boundaries is built into the web. What walls do you want to break down?

[1] The Cluetrain Manifesto.

The fact that we can read firsthand the tweets and blog posts of bloggers in Iran or China, and can read the tweets and Facebook updates of people involved in the Arab Spring is revolutionary. We have never had this capacity before. Sure the telephone connected people around the world and television brings pictures from afar, but this is different. This is mass but it is also in our control, it is personal, it is asynchronous and distributed all at the same time. It allows us to experience the world as joined up as never before. We are all becoming more aware that actions cause reactions. You might find that you have more in common with someone on the other side of the world than with the person in the house next door.

So we can cross geographical and political boundaries with relative ease for the first time, but inside organizations there are still significant boundaries keeping us apart. People separate themselves by department, by status, or by role. It is not easy to instigate a conversation between people in different silos within the same organizations. Even if you are in the same, or related, parts of the business you are often physically separated – either by being in a different building or even in a different corner of a large open plan office. You can be isolated in a room full of people.

Shrinking these gaps that inevitably appear between us has all sorts of business benefits. We can help solve each other's problems if we know we have them. We can make better decisions if we know what is happening "around us". We can make more effective use of a resource if more people share it and we can do this only if we have an easy way of coordinating our activities. Knowing that there is someone else out there in your organization facing the same problems that you are, or able to help you solve yours, is not easy, but it is the first step to reducing a lot of the seemingly inevitable inefficiency that drags us down.

Crossing these boundaries and seeing into other people's worlds can raise challenges too though. I remember someone once asking on a forum what the organization's policy for claiming expenses on using your own car for business purposes was. The first thing that happened was that about half a dozen people offered different answers. You can imagine some managers disapproving of them all "misinforming each other". But when you think of it the tool wasn't causing the misinformation – it was just revealing that it existed. Each person had offered what they thought was the right answer. Indeed without the forum they would have gone on thinking that what they thought was the right answer. However, what happened soon after was that someone responded to the question by linking to the HR document that explained the policy. This meant that everyone got to know (a) that there was a policy and (b) where the policy was. Without the forum and this question we may never have known of its existence and struggled to find it on the intranet – a thankless task at the best of times.

What happened next was that a couple of people came back and said "Well, we know that that is the official position – but our bit of the business interprets it differently because . . ." and then went on to describe why the policy, as written, didn't make sense in their part of the business. Initially this sort of thing could feel like HR's worst nightmare but in fact it was of real value to them. They got to learn that their policy – which they probably assumed was universally applicable – wasn't. They now had the opportunity to do something about this whereas without the forum they would have been none the wiser.

Let's take another scenario. Imagine that industrial unrest in one part of an organization is picked up online and mimicked in another. This is probably a more testing case for managers where the possibility of mass insurrection rears its ugly head. But if you have encouraged and developed a demographically representative online community, with a strong culture of responsible behaviour, you have little to worry about. If you have a strong case for your position then those causing trouble will have to deal with their colleagues who believe they are acting unreasonably. If you have the courage to wait until these types of things have the time to sort themselves out, they invariably do.

On the other hand, if you have a big enough problem for it to surface in more than one part of your organization then you really do have a problem. If this is the case it is probably as well that you deal with it rather than hide from it. If the problems have the capacity to spread quickly so do the solutions. The management team have the same tools at their disposal as do the staff. Remember we are all individual nodes in the network and our power as such is dependent on our ability to persuade others. This may seem scary and radical but it is also enabling. You are able to see dissent and do something about it quickly. Isn't this better than not knowing it's there and getting caught out by it when it is too late?

All organizations talk about their organizational culture but how is that culture established and protected? Global outsourcing, mergers, acquisitions, and re-structuring are all increasingly common aspects of our work lives. If you have a merger situation, very little is done to accommodate the coming together of often very different cultures. Old networks can be blown apart and new ones thrown together. The ongoing churn of organizational change can be pretty brutal and the bonds that hold organizations together can become very stretched as a result of the upheaval. When there is less time, less tolerance, and less shared spaces, having a way to create cohesion and a strong corporate culture online can be a huge advantage. People who are dispersed and remote from centres of power can still have influence. People who don't do well face to face can have influence. People from different organizational tribes and cultures can rub virtual shoulders with one another. Even when separated by distance or physical barriers, online conversations can be a powerful management tool if used well. It is possible to build a robust, shared, corporate culture entirely online and this may well become the main way that we maintain cohesion in the face of increasing instability in the future.

When we were in the middle of building our networks inside the BBC I was asked to come up with a one-sentence job description for my boss. I suggested "Increasing the quality and frequency of the conversations that get your job done". I thought this was pretty good. Work focused, and self-explanatory. However I was told that the word conversation wasn't businesslike enough – even though what I was talking about was the willingness to informally share knowledge with each other. I still reckon that that sentence is a good summation of what we are talking about throughout this book.

Someone once said that the conversations on our forum at the BBC had done more to foster a "one BBC culture" than any of the grandiose internal communications initiatives of the same name. But we did it ourselves, one conversation at a time. Rubbing shoulders virtually and helping each other online. Isn't this how culture always works? Isn't this how culture changes?

These are not "just" conversations for the sake of conversations. They are conversations that help us to understand the world around us and to deal effectively with the challenges it presents us. We have these conversations together, one at a time, and by doing so build our shared culture. Making it easier to have these conversations and allowing more people to take part in them is an exciting new way for managers to engage with the organizations they manage. Getting good at it will be the way to establish the robust cultures that will be necessary to succeed in the unpredictable world we increasingly inhabit.

Things to remember:

- Use the web to help people connect across geographical, political . . . and organizational barriers.
- If we can cross barriers and share problems we have a chance to work on them together.
- Being able to connect with others in your organization, without having to be in the same space at the same time, allows us to share and help solve each other's problems.
- Visible conversations surface problems and this gives us the chance to deal with them.
- Conversations aren't trivial. Culture is reinforced by shared conversations and understanding.

19

CONVERSATIONS CAN ONLY TAKE PLACE BETWEEN EQUALS

So if conversations are such a big part of our ability to succeed, why are we so bad at them in business? Why have we professionalized our conversations to such an extent that we have forgotten how to speak normally to one another? Why do we have one conversation with our peers and another with our staff? Have we lost the art of conversation and if so how can we get it back?

David Weinberger's insight that "conversations can only take place between equals" is key to what we are talking about here. So key that it deserves its own chapter. What I believe he is saying is that if two people are not prepared to see each other as equal, at least for the duration of their interaction with each other, then what they are having is not a conversation. If one of them is the boss, and acts like it, this is not a conversation – it is a broadcast. If the other is too scared to be open and say what they think – it is not a conversation. If one is aware of being superior in any way and is not interested in really listening – it is not a conversation. If one is a corporation and one is a customer – it is not a conversation. Given that we are saying that the Internet enables "globally distributed, near instant, person to person, conversations", this matters.

These distinctions persist online. If one half of a conversation is a well known blogger with thousands of followers and the other is a newbie – and if they both act like it – this isn't a conversation. If one is a Generation Y new recruit who knows all the online conventions and the other is a manager old enough to be their parent – and if both act like it – this is not a conversation. If one is talking management speak and the other is talking street – this is not a conversation. On the other hand, if both parties are relaxed, confident, and willing to go with the flow as they chuck ideas back and forth, then it is a conversation.

So why does this matter? The point of social tools is being able to work things out as we go and in collaboration with others. It is about a flexible approach to change. Being open to new ideas and refining old ones is why we do it. If we want to do this together we will need to establish more equable relationships. The benefits of increased collaboration and sharing of knowledge won't emerge unless people are relaxed, confident, and trust each other enough to be open.

As a result of these possibilities the demands on managers are changing. They won't be able to rely on authority to get things done. Rather than being able to protect themselves with management speak, and resort to status as a protection, they will have to learn to open up and have a totally new form of engagement. The best managers will be the ones who make people feel comfortable and trusted. They will be the ones who ask the best questions. They will be the ones who are prepared to be vulnerable and admit that they don't know all the answers.

Informality will feel uncomfortable for many at first but they will get over it – and it will feel like a blessed relief for many. At a conference recently a couple of younger IT directors praised me for having the confidence to wear jeans in a business setting. I said it was a deliberate policy of mine to avoid the besuited uniform of most managers. I do this because it reflects my desire to minimize the differences between me and the people I am talking to. It may seem a trivial point but there is no advantage in resting on ceremony while preaching relaxed communication between equals. At another conference I was approached by a manager in a suit who was disparaging of these arguments and said it took more than not wearing a suit to bring about change. He was right, but he simply told me this was true – we didn't have a conversation!

Now no one is saying that everyone in business is equal. For the foreseeable future we will continue to have varying levels of skill, responsibility, and reward. But in terms of "the network" we are equal. There is no top or bottom, middle or edge. There are just nodes – and everyone has the same opportunity to be an important node that adds value – or not. We all have an interest in the network working. We all have an interest in the diverse voices being heard. If there is a difference in the network it is between those nodes that contribute freely and help information flow more readily – and those that don't.

There has been a lot written about the end of hierarchies. In fact David Weinberger also wrote that "hyperlinks subvert hierarchies". But do we really mean this? Don't hierarchies emerge everywhere in human nature? Won't there be some who take to blogging and tweeting more readily than others and therefore end up on top of a new pile? Perhaps, but it is likely to be a more temporary ascendancy to the top of the pile – because the pile keeps moving and morphing into other piles. What is much more likely to emerge is an ephemeral meritocracy. You will gain status, and therefore power, if you add value to a lot of people. But don't expect it to last. Don't attempt to freeze it and institutionalize it. Someone else will add more value tomorrow, and the moving anthill of conversations will move on. The networks of individuals will reshape around the new conversations and those who are adding value will change.

What will create lasting influence is your willingness to go with this process. Being willing to help others, allowing power to move away from you, ignoring your position and status to enable people to have real and productive conversations with you will be the way to gain power and influence in the future. I haven't seen a better case of "the more you give out the more you get back" philosophy than on the web. The golden rule applies in a space where Google, or your colleagues, never forget. Good karma will mean more than prestigious job titles. Having helped others will be your best guarantee of support when you are needing them to help you. Being seen to help others will be the most effective way to gain influence – at least for a while. "Management by being interested" will become the norm. Being willing to go with this ebb and flow of influence will give you more power than trying to stand in the way of the wave.

Things to remember:

- Conversations only take place when people are willing to see themselves as equal for the duration of the encounter.
- Only when people trust each other and feel comfortable with sharing with each other will we see the true benefits of the networked world.
- Managers will be less able to rely on formal authority and will achieve influence through the quality of their relationships.
- Status doesn't go away with online networks but the behaviours that support it change.
- Ephemeral meritocracies will take the place of many hierarchies as status and power become more fluid.
- The more you give out the more you get back has never been truer, or more obvious, than online.

20

MANAGEMENT BY BEING INTERESTED

Managers' authority is being replaced by the need to influence, so how will they manage in the future? How do you manage online environments and encourage them to be a productive use of people's time? Being obsessively interested in what people are doing and asking great questions is the way to help steer their collective energy towards successful outcomes.

Let's assume for the moment that you have built a suite of online tools, either for your staff or customers, in which people are beginning to be actively engaged in talking about their work, their challenges, their opportunities, and their solutions. They are beginning to think for themselves and work out together what to do about things. But there are also people not using the tools and sometimes those who do get into unproductive behaviours or cause tension and dissent. How do you deal with this? What do you do to help the network figure out how to work well? You have stuck your neck out and got the tools installed – what if they don't work? What if things go wrong? Perhaps the hardest hurdle to overcome is having faith in people and expecting your users to have the capacity to make this thing work with the right help.

People used to think that no one did anything until told to by management and there is still a culture in many organizations of doing the minimum possible and staying safe. The assumption was that we needed to be directed and without that direction, would be unproductive. This idea never really made sense as we all manage to be self-directing to some extent in our lives outside work. This assumption that people won't work without direction seems even more suspect when anyone can now see groups of people getting together and helping each other online to achieve amazing and complex things – and often for no apparent reason. The most widely known example of this is the open source software movement. This doesn't have managers in the conventional sense, though it is not unmanaged, and people will get together to solve each other's problems unprompted by a higher authority. Structures and roles emerge to make things work but there is no predetermined managerial chain of command.

As these types of online environments become more common in business with more people taking responsibility for themselves and their actions, the role of those in charge is more crucial than ever. If there is an online group that is working well together and establishing new ways of working with each other, having someone wade in and tell them what to do, exercising conventional authority, can do a lot of damage. Especially if you are a manager you need to be very wary of the impact you can have. People know that you have more power than they have and you have disproportionate impact. If you are going to intervene in online conversations in what might seem to others an arbitrary and high handed fashion, they will learn not to do anything before you do. They will not risk heading in a particular direction until they have seen how you are going to react. By being online this situation is different from conventional management challenges because everyone is watching. Your impact goes beyond those you are talking to. Even if they are not directly involved in this particular situation, others can see how you react. Your actions are amplified, their consequences have more impact, and everyone learns to wait.

So if I am right and you don't need to manage people as much as you think – how do you make things happen when making things happen is seen as a bad thing?

Firstly you need to get people used to thinking for themselves. You have to give them the space to take responsibility. When we were getting our forum up and running at the BBC, I gave people almost complete autonomy over the platform. I needed them to use it and really didn't care what they used it for, so long as it became thriving and active – which it would only do if it had some utility for them. This may seem an extreme position – like laissez faire taken to its limits – but I knew that if they didn't use the tools then the tools would die. By taking ownership people populated the spaces and learned how to use them. They used them for whatever made sense to them and this meant that there were people who knew what to do when real work issues became the focus for our energies.

During this process there were times when things appeared to be going wrong – when things were getting tense or when threads dried up and went quiet. On those occasions I felt a strong pressure to do something, to come up with answers, to tell people what to do, or even to decide for them the meaning of what was happening. But if you do this, people learn to expect you to react and for you to tell them what is happening and why. So you learn to wait. Sometimes for what seems like an unbearably long time. You wait until the users start to sort out situations themselves. Maybe a particular member steps in and resolves a situation, or a group decides amongst themselves what is right and wrong and what they are going to do about it. They do this because they have been given the space to take responsibility. This takes skill and strength.

Does this mean you give up trying to manage? Well for one thing it doesn't mean you are giving up all responsibility. You are probably at least nominally responsible for these online spaces. If anything went seriously wrong it would be your neck on the block. So in fact you have to be involved in steering what happens all the time – but in unconventional ways.

The most powerful of these is to be intensely interested in what is happening. It is fascinating, and indeed a privilege, to watch a large group of people work out, largely for themselves, what these things are, and what we can all do with them. Most tools make it easy to subscribe to every thread on every topic and even with a system that involves 25,000 users, such as we had at the BBC, this means around 400 emails a day. This seems like a lot but you get used to knowing the signs to look out for and it allows you to keep track of what is happening, what people are doing, who is active, and where there is any tension. Once you realize something is going on, you watch to see how people are reacting and how they are sorting things for themselves. Sometimes you have to ask a question to get the ball rolling. "This is interesting – there seems to be something going on here. What do we think it is? Is it good or bad? Are we happy with keeping on doing it or do we need to do something else? If we stop doing it what would we do instead?"

These simple questions will invariably kick off great discussions of what people are doing and why, thus enabling some incredibly effective group learning. And of course it isn't just the active participants in the debate who learn. With any luck you will have thousands and thousands of staff who watch what is happening in your online spaces even if they don't take part. Being a "lurker" isn't as bad as it sounds and lurkers learn a lot as well! You can direct the attention of a lot of people towards solving problems and learning from each other by the simple fact of being interested and learning to ask good questions. Be careful though because, especially in the early days, this is risky work. Admitting to being interested makes you feel vulnerable. It looks and feels as if the people who work for you know better than you. The big news is that they often do! You can't fake this approach to management and you won't get away with it if your interest isn't genuine. If you ask insincere or "management speak" questions, the regulars will at best ignore you, and at worst attack. But if you have a good grasp of what is interesting and why, people will learn to trust your instincts and follow your attention.

But isn't this too passive? Don't managers have to tell people what to do? Won't people just sit back and do nothing unless directed? I often get push back on this with the comment "But surely it takes more than being interested to motivate people? People want to get through their days with the minimum effort, collect their money and go." Is that really true? Isn't that how we have been trained to be? What if we were trained differently? What if your manager showed you that they really valued your perspective and found you interesting – rather than paying lip service to the idea? People are not used to management finding what they do interesting. Not genuinely interesting on a personal level. Once people see that you are paying attention to their online activities, and that you are genuinely interested in the whole thing working for everyone, they will respond. They will respond really positively to your questions and join in the collective learning process.

Where you place your attention matters in life generally but nowhere more so than in a large online forum. In fact it is all about focusing our attention. What is working, what is not? Who is doing interesting things? Where are people feeling uneasy and why? What should we be doing in this situation? Is this happening anywhere else? By being genuinely interested and asking questions you can gently steer the attention of large groups of people. By steering attention you focus energy, and the focused energy of interested people invariably starts to improve things. The better you get at asking good questions the more influence you will have and the more effectively you will be able to manage your online spaces.

Things to remember:

- You need to be very sensitive to your impact in online spaces and how people react to your interventions.
- If you keep telling people what to do and how to act they will learn to wait for you to do so.
- Give people the space and confidence to begin to take responsibility for their online spaces.
- Really pay attention to what is happening and help others to understand by sharing what you find interesting.
- You are not giving up your responsibility as a manager but are exercising it differently.
- Learn to ask really good questions that help steer people towards better solutions or deeper understanding.

21

ASKING THE RIGHT QUESTIONS

Knowing all the answers isn't as easy as it used to be and maybe we should stop trying. Learning to ask the right questions is the way to help people move forwards and get better at sorting their own problems.

How often have you ever really needed your boss to tell you what to do? You might need him to give you some context and some background information, but in terms of what you actually do you really don't want him sitting on your shoulder telling you your every move. People don't want you to tell them what to do as much as they used to. Increasingly you get things to happen by asking good questions.

In the past, in a command and control world, it was assumed that you got things to happen by telling people what to do. The higher up the chain you moved, the more people you got to tell what to do. You were expected to know more than those below you, and to be the one with the most experience and knowledge. This allowed you to make the best decisions about what was to be done, by whom, and why. This was a scary place to be at the best of times and it is becoming increasingly unrealistic. The world is complicated and moving ever faster. People's expectations are changing. We need to shift our assumptions about how to manage people and move away from notions of being in charge and towards working out collectively what makes us more effective.

This shift in assumptions is even more obvious online. The range of people able to share their knowledge can be huge and how you help them to do so is changing. You can't expect to throw your weight around as an expert or a manager – you have to work with the community to help it work towards its own answers. Your online forum will never take off and won't survive for very long if you adopt a conventional command and control approach. People have to work out for themselves what is going on, why, and how they feel about it. They don't need anyone to tell them.

So as a manager, you should resist the temptation to leap in and start "sorting" things. You know, the old way of doing things by deciding what is going wrong and being the hero by coming in and fixing it. One of my staff who had been very involved in counselling told me a wonderful phrase which captures this risk for me, which is: "to rescue someone is to oppress them". In other words, by saying people are broken and need fixing – and you are the person to fix them – you keep people in their broken state. It gives power to the fixer and the person being fixed knows this. The same rule applies to online conversations. By wading in with the right answer to every situation you risk killing any feelings of community stone dead.

So how do you influence things if you are not allowed to know all of the answers or tell people what to do? You do it by asking good questions. If you see something that is causing tension, you could ask questions such as:

"Is there something going on here?"
"Has anyone else noticed that things seem unusual?"
"What do we feel about what is happening – is it good or bad?"
"If it is bad do we need to do anything about it?"
"What are we going to do?"
"What would help?"
"What did we do the last time?"

By asking these questions you invite people to engage with the solution. You encourage them to take responsibility and to do so together. Asking questions can generate energy. You can tap into people's natural curiosity and help them to surface and share what they know – but you do it in a very enabling way. Even if you write statements, say for example in a post on your blog, you can write them in such a way as to imply a question, to invite ongoing debate. Asking questions is very empowering. You are calling on the person to actively engage in their workplace and its challenges and expecting them to be willing and able to move things forward. It is this sense of shared, collective responsibility that allows people to take care of themselves and each other.

Having asked a question you have to be prepared to listen to the answer. This may seem like stating the blindingly obvious but it rarely happens. It takes real effort to listen – even online – but if you don't you might as well not bother asking questions in the first place. In fact if you are seen not to listen or really care what the answers are then people will tire of offering answers to them. Remember that your lack of real listening is potentially being seen by your whole organization or the wider world. Be really interested in the answers and let people see this. Even if you are making statements, there is a way to do this that opens up the conversation rather than closing it down.

One of the things I am most proud of on my blog is the number and the quality of the comments. I write in a way that hopefully indicates that I don't think I have all of the answers, and even if I make statements they are there as a starter for ten rather than the definitive answer. There is a knack to writing like this and it is a very powerful way to foster connections with people. Asking good questions and being good at listening to the answers are amongst the most powerful and empowering things you can do. These are not soft, new age skills either. This is about collectively establishing the best solutions and most effective ways of working in a fast moving and complex world.

Things to remember:

- Knowing all the answers is an increasingly impossible expectation.
- People rarely need to be told what to do but sometimes need help working it out.
- Resist the temptation to act as if you know all the answers and get good at asking great questions instead.
- Focus attention and energy by asking the right questions at the right time.
- Be prepared to listen to the answers!
- Listening is hard work and is a skill that needs practice.

22

THE MEANING OF TRUE COLLABORATION

Every corporation says it values collaboration and wants to encourage more of it. Almost every piece of enterprise software claims to support collaboration somehow. But what does collaboration mean? What does it look like when it happens? How do we do it? How does the web help us do it better?

Collaboration is one of those big words isn't it? Many of us use it, especially in business. It gets bandied around quite a lot. On the other hand, you don't find staff using the word much. They just do stuff together. Collaboration is a bit like innovation, creativity, and engagement – words that have been hijacked and had their meaning misappropriated. You see people sharing documents with each other, having email exchanges, and talking to each other on the phone but how much of this is truly collaborative? Isn't a lot of it simply sharing information?

When people are in places they feel comfortable in, with people they feel comfortable with, they might just start talking together about things that matter to them or things that they are trying to achieve. This is the essence of collaboration – low level conversations carried out in the process of doing stuff – "conversations that get your job done". We sort of know what this feels like and intuitively know that more of it would be a good thing. The trouble is that as soon as you start to orchestrate it, or measure it, or demand more of it – it tends to evaporate. This problem is even more acute when people try to take this collaboration idea and make it into tools. There is a lot of "collaboration software" out there that is really just the same stuff that failed to deliver data management, information management, knowledge management and is now failing to deliver collaboration. In fact a lot of the tools labelled as collaboration tools actually work against effective collaboration.

The mindset is wrong and the design of the tools makes the emergence of true collaboration less likely. These tools are often chosen centrally, forced upon the staff, and then their owners attempt to manage which conversations are allowed, and where you are allowed to have them. This rarely works. Collaboration is subtler than this. It happens in more serendipitous ways. People are much more sophisticated about how they collaborate, when, and with whom. This is why an ecology of different low cost tools is much more likely to succeed than enterprise scale tools and the command and control culture that tends to come with them.

So how do you act collaboratively? You have to be open to other people helping you. You have to be prepared to ask for help. You also have to be prepared to listen to the help that is offered and to possibly then do something with it. These challenges can be made easier in the online world. You can more easily find people to collaborate with who are trying to solve the same problems as you or who know something that can help you solve your problem. You can strike up a conversation with them even if you don't know them or aren't able to meet face to face. If you use the tools to work together and share knowledge, what you have done is automatically recorded and findable by others. Those who find you can then chip in with their own contributions or make a connection with you and join in.

You can spread your collaboration through much larger groups online than would be practical normally. Look at some of the large, complex, open source projects that can involve hundreds of people dispersed around the world bouncing ideas off each other and working on solving problems together 24/7. Being able to collaborate asynchronously is new too. The fact that not only do you not have to be in the same place to collaborate but you don't even have to be working at the same time of day. The to and fro of microblogging tools like Twitter, or the asynchronous contributions to a wiki like Wikipedia, allow people to have a constructive dialogue as they work on problems. These dialogues can be snatched windows of communication spread over hours or days but that nonetheless retain the thread of a conversation.

Being seen to be open to collaboration and generating the right culture matters. One of the first things people comment on when they start to engage online is the willingness of other people to go out of their way to help. There is a generosity and a willingness to get involved that is rare in the offline business world. I first saw this back in 1995 when my wife and I were visiting Canada on holiday. We wanted to find out about the best ferries to get from Vancouver to Vancouver Island. I asked the question on Usenet, an early precursor of the groups and forums now built into Facebook and LinkedIn. I posted my question on alt.rec. travel.canada.misc and got several detailed answers back from people I would never meet and all within moments. These answers then kicked off conversations that allowed me to work with these people I would never meet to solve my problem. You can see examples of this every day in the thousands of intranet forums that now exist in businesses around the world. People going out of their way to help each other and doing so using simple tools that rarely have the word collaboration written on them.

True collaboration is a succession of these small examples of the willingness to help another person. The motivation for doing so is universal but it can be fragile and can be lost in an instant. Collaboration is one of those things that is difficult to mandate. It has to be willingly engaged in. Sure you can build processes and rules that make it obligatory that people pass bits of information on to one another in a chain, but this isn't really what collaboration is about. Collaboration is a shared willingness to address problems or opportunities and often to contribute hard won personal experience to doing so. You want there to be as few barriers to collaboration as possible. It is almost always a cognitive overhead and anything that makes it harder or more complicated than it should be is going to make it less likely to happen. Don't turn collaboration into an initiative but do make it easier to do. Don't talk about doing it but instead increase the frequency and quality of those conversations that get your job done.

Things to remember:

- Collaboration is much slipperier and harder to encourage than software vendors would have you believe.
- People have to feel comfortable and trust each other before they will go out of their way to collaborate.
- Don't turn collaboration into a big thing and don't try to manage it in conventional ways.
- Make sure your tools encourage flexibility and share responsibility. They need to make it easier rather than harder to collaborate.
- Tap into the willingness to help each other and work together on problems that is so often seen on the Internet. Create the right circumstances for this behaviour to grow.
- Encourage a shared willingness to help others by doing it rather than talking about it.

23

WAR OF THE WORLDS

We talk as if online exists in isolation from the rest of our lives but of course it doesn't. It becomes intertwined with our face to face encounters and the trick is to get the best of both worlds.

The online world doesn't exist in isolation from the "real" world. In fact let's deal with that word "real" for a moment. It always has air quotes with it when being discussed by those used to spending time online. The assumption that our physical world is more real than our online world is problematic. I would argue that the relationships we establish with each other online are no less real than those we have face to face. In many ways we get to know each other better online through more open and thoughtful written exchanges than would be acceptable in a casual office conversation. I feel as if I know people I have known online for years, but have never met face to face, better than people I shared an office with for years. We can also spend a lot of time sharing the same physical space with another person and hardly know them at all.

There are benefits to the Internet that are different from some aspects of our physical realities. On the Internet you are as good as the ideas you express and your willingness to help others. No one cares, or will possibly ever know, whether you are tall or small, good looking or average. This non-physical world will have its own elites but they are less likely to be based on physical appearance. Equally there are lots of downsides to face to face. People can make assumptions about you based on your appearance, dress, and other outward signs of status. This shift towards online has a powerful effect, and increasingly conditions our relationships with each other. Managing the transition between these two worlds is something we will get better at and will be seen as a key business and personal skill.

But of course, as with so many things, this is not a question of either/or. I love face to face. In fact I am very aware that I only have so much face to face time available to me on the planet and I have an interest in making the best use of it that I can. This is where the online tools help. Thanks to an upfront investment in time building online networks,

I get to spend more of my face to face time with really interesting people, having really useful conversations, than I ever have before.

This is where geo location applications like Foursquare come in. These tools pick up on the GPS signal in our phones and then alert our social networks as to where we are. People often wonder why those of us who use the tools spend time telling people where we are. Aren't we worried about people breaking into our houses when we have broadcast the fact that we are elsewhere? God bless the media for making us so paranoid. The reason I like people to know my location is because it means I get to meet more interesting people. As an example, when I arrived in Washington recently for a conference, Foursquare automatically updated my Twitter stream with my location. People who follow me in that area knew I was in town and as a result of that, a major in the US Army bought me lunch and I was shown round The Smithsonian by one of its curators! Neither of these very pleasant and useful face to face meetings would have happened if the tools hadn't announced the fact that I was in town.

As with so many things though, you can have too much of a good thing. Be careful not to pollute your Twitter stream with too many location updates – people will soon turn you off. In other cases, it may not be appropriate to let people know where you are. Sometimes I work with organizations where just knowing my location would give away who I am working with. Many clients wouldn't be happy at the opportunity this would give people to put two and two together and to make assumptions about the reasons that I was doing business with them.

But it is in the blending together of online and offline that the real benefits can be seen. Online conversations in the workplace don't stay online for long. News that is spread, or topics that are discussed on an intranet forum, will soon be discussed in corridors and in meetings. I would often be stopped on my way from one office to another by people who I had been chatting with online. Even though I may not have met them before "in the flesh", we were able to pick up our conversations and continue them as if we had known each other for years.

As you begin to use online tools more in your business you will notice changes. When you have a meeting, half of the attendees are probably users of those online tools and they turn up with lots of shared contextual information, common ground, and agreement because they have already been engaged with each other and the topic of the meeting online. The other half of the meeting, who aren't active online, will look blank and start the laborious and time consuming process of catching up. They won't get away with continuing to do this for long. There was always, and always will be, a percentage of the work population who don't take part in these online conversations but they will come under increasing pressure to do so.

Over time our buildings and their architecture will also start to change as a result of our use of these online tools. As we spend more time talking, thinking, and working together online, we will need physical spaces for different reasons. We will hopefully need the work PC tethered to the work desk less and less but we will need more places to meet up with those we know online. Rather than staring at each other across the sea of desks in an open plan office we will want to get together briefly for quality face to face time. We will have different types of meetings for different reasons. Our time "at work" will be differently defined and our desire to travel to a physical place to have a face to face meeting will change. I am not one of those that sell the idea that online removes the need for face to face. The amount of my own air travel is testimony to this. But I do think the reasons we meet face to face will change, the productivity of such meetings will increase, and yes, some of the issues we currently feel the need to have a meeting for will be dealt with in other ways.

To be productive in the future we will need to make better decisions as to where to spend our time and what to do in either the virtual or the physical worlds that we will increasingly move between. Working out when a blog post, a comment on a forum, a phone call, an email, or a face to face meeting is the right thing to do for the best result. The skill will be in managing the transitions. We will need to be thoughtful about our use of physical or digital space and take responsibility for using them to best effect.

Things to remember:

- The online world is different from the offline world but no less real.
- There are advantages to both the online and the offline worlds.
- Letting people know where we are, or are going to be, increases the opportunities for serendipitous face to face meetings.
- Blending online conversations with offline ones is very productive and more and more people are seeing the business benefits.
- As we use more tools to communicate remotely our need for space won't go away altogether but it will change.
- Managing the transitions between online and offline will be key. We need to get good at making the right decisions as to where we spend our time and how.

24

THE INSIDE IS BECOMING THE OUTSIDE

There used to be a clear distinction between being at work and not. The edges of organizations used to be clear and fixed. Nowadays you can be at work anywhere and your staff might be talking about their work all over the web. How do you make this an opportunity rather than a threat?

In the old days you had to travel from home to your place of work and your work environment had a distinct edge through which you had to pass. You wore different clothes at work than you did at home and very probably used different language. There was a security guard at the door who checked on your right to enter and once through, you were expected to know how to behave appropriately.

The Internet changes this. We can now be "at work" anywhere and at any time. The distinctions between work and non-work have become very blurred. In fact even within the environment of your computer what is work and what is not has become blurred. It used to be that your Microsoft Office suite of tools was your workplace, but increasingly our browsers are our workplaces. If we are accessing forums and blogs and wikis for work purposes we do so through the browser just as we do if we are accessing them for non-work purposes. Web tools are invading the workplace and we use networking sites for work and social purposes interchangeably.

Even in technological terms the line between work and non-work is getting softer. The firewall that separates us from the outside world means nothing if we are using our smartphone at home and at work. More and more of us access the Internet on mobile devices even if these are not officially sanctioned or provided. I was with a senior HR manager recently who, with a twinkle in her eye, pointed to her business PC and her smartphone sitting side by side on her desk and said "which do you think I use all day?"

This blurring of the inside and the outside raises issues both for us as individuals and the organizations we work for. For us it means that we have to take more responsibility for whatever lines we draw between work and non-work. We have to work harder at deciding what we do where and when. We may have to make more effort to communicate those decisions to our managers or our partners. We can't *not* make these decisions, and they will have an increasing impact on the quality of our lives. For our organizations this is even more critical. When are we working for an organization and when are we not? How do those we work for make sure that they can trust us to behave appropriately? Control used to be exercised through access to the tools for the job, but as we have seen, we now have access to these all of the time. When most of us only had access to computers at work, our activities could be monitored – this is not so easy to do when we are working in the nearest Starbucks on our own iPad.

There are upsides to the inside becoming more connected to the outside in terms of connections with our customers too. The barriers between those who work in an organization and its customers are falling. It is easier to strike up a genuine conversation with a customer than ever before, or to connect with people working in the businesses that serve yours. In fact we are all customers of our own and each other's services and pervasive online conversations make this ever more apparent.

So how do we all manage this transition from the inside to the outside? The only way is through communication, influence, and trust. We have to work out together what appropriate behaviour is, at what times, and in which circumstances. Employees and employers have to work together to redraw the lines of the employment contract. Those people working closer to the edges are often going faster than those at the centre but we all have an interest in helping each other to catch up. Maintaining control when things are as new and as fast changing as they are at the moment is a challenge. Loose networks of people coming and going and connecting for different reasons at different times and in different places requires a very different way of thinking about the organizations we work for.

It also calls for a different way of managing people. Rather than having rigid rules you have to help people understand what their responsibilities are and how they carry them out. We will all get better at managing how we have these conversations and knowing what is effective and productive in which circumstances. The world of work will be less distinct from the other worlds we inhabit, but it will be increasingly possible to manage the transitions between these various worlds more smoothly than we do currently.

Things to remember:

- Whereas many of us used to rely on technology provided by work to get things done, we can increasingly work anywhere we choose and often using our own tools.
- There used to be a clear demarcation between work and non-work. The line between the two is becoming blurred.
- There will be more responsibility placed on individuals to manage when they are at work and when not.
- Online conversations are taking place between staff and customers. Working out what is appropriate where and when will take more thought.
- We need to learn how to conduct our online conversations appropriately and manage the transitions between the inside and the outside of our businesses.

25

YOUR STAFF ARE YOUR BEST ADVOCATES

Much of marketing in the past has been about maintaining a brand image and paying professional marketeers and PR professionals to do this for us. Social media offers the possibility of finding our own voices and having real conversations with real customers.

Much of the public use of social media by corporations up until now has been by marketing. In fact the phrase has come to mean a subset of what is possible with the social web and has to some extent become devalued as a result. I have deliberately avoided that bias in this book partly in an attempt to address the imbalance but also because I believe that helping organizations, or those who work for them, to find their own voice, or voices, is the best way to connect to their customers.

I believe that marketing and PR are professions at real risk of disintermediation by the web. We will need people to do our marketing for us less and less as we use the tools in everyday work and start to have more effective conversations between ourselves and our customers. Likewise PR. As the stories in the news move gradually online and become more distributed in nature, the idea of paying someone else to manage your story for you will become progressively alien. This doesn't mean that we won't need help – but the nature of the help we need will change. Rather than wanting someone to do our storytelling and marketing for us, we will want them to help us tell our own stories better.

I have been around marketing enough over the past few years to anticipate the cries of "but this is already what we do – help people to tell their stories". My experience and observation is that they don't. They get in the middle and get in the way. They make what might be a compelling story sound false and make the possibility of a real relationship between company and client a remote possibility. They are middle men getting in between customers and the businesses they want to relate to. Instead of taking someone's message and mangling it, in the future they will help them to tell it better. Help them to find their voice. Help them to learn the ropes online faster and make mistakes less painfully. Become a trusted source of advice and support rather than doing people's talking for them.

So how do you use these tools to market effectively? I am no marketing expert, and make no pretence about that, but there are some things that do seem glaringly obvious and in fact resonate with much of what I have been saying throughout this book. Listen first. Really listen. Listen to the good and the bad, no matter who is saying it or where they are saying it. This is the first time you have had the possibility to get this close to customers and prospects. Do your own listening. Don't outsource it and read bland reports.

Require all staff and managers to learn how to find and listen to conversations about your products or services online. Get them to listen to what is being said and share it with everyone else in the company who is interested. Help them to connect to the people they are listening to. Help your staff to become your best advocates. Give them the tools and the insights to become your ambassadors online. Treat the relationships that emerge with respect. Don't consign them to a faceless database. Try to maintain the connection despite personnel and industry changes. Do whatever you can to keep the conversation going at an appropriate level with everyone who has trusted you enough to open up a conversation with you.

As I write this I can again feel marketing teams taking it in but assimilating it into the same old same old, muttering that this kind of connection doesn't scale. Well then maybe your company doesn't scale. Maybe you are too big for me to relate to and build a trusting relationship with. Maybe this is the new upper limit to critical mass. If the quality of the relationship between a company and its customers defines success in the marketplace, and being a large corporate means that you can't foster trust with your clients, then maybe you will crumble under your own weight. Maybe your competitors who manage their relationships better will steal away your clients. Hasn't business always been about relationships – haven't markets always been conversations?

In the future we will expect companies to know us, know our interests, know our needs, and even know us as people a little bit. We are all sharing demographic, geographic, and every other 'graphic' information about ourselves online in an outbreak of openness never seen before. The companies who learn how to make the most of this information, while crucially maintaining our trust, will be the ones who win business in the future. The added value will be context. Getting the right product, in the right way, at the right time, and for the right price, will become the new standard. In fact I may even pay you a premium for getting me – more quickly and cost effectively – to buy products that I don't even know about until you tell me.

This is a million miles away from the sort of very broadly targeted marketing we are subject to currently. In fact the words such as campaign, blitz, target etc. that we use to describe marketing campaigns should be a warning sign. We are treating our customers like our enemies and they know it. Treat me right and I will let you into my life and I will allow you to use up some of my valuable cognitive surplus to whisper in my ear about products and services that I don't even know I need yet. Abuse my trust and I will drop you in the blink of an eye, use recommendations from my network to find a viable alternative, and slag you off online for all to see.

Markets are most definitely conversations and with appropriate use of social tools we can allow the conversations taking place inside our organizations to reach out through the firewall to connect with our customers. The whole point of all of this is to make it easier to add value to each other in ways that make sense, are effective, and make the world a better place. Having staff more connected and collectively accountable inside the business should lead to more effective businesses. Taking the next step and connecting them with customers should lead to greater satisfaction. Call me a naïve optimist if you like, and I know that this scenario is a million miles away from where we are now, but it is a really good place to aspire to getting to!

Things to remember:

- Marketing and PR have hijacked the phrase "social media" and it has come to mean a subset of what is possible with the tools.
- We have professionalized our connections with customers to such a degree that we are losing connection altogether.
- Markets are conversations. Real brand and real trust come through these conversations.
- If you are too big to maintain real conversations with real people, maybe you are too big to survive?
- Social tools let us have better conversations with companies about the things we need or want. This will increase our chances of getting what we want when we want it.
- Building real relationships is the best way to build real business and real brands.

26

CREATIVELY MESSY

Is creativity the preserve of the few or an untapped possibility for the many? The messiness of the web enables the origination and dissemination of wonderful examples of creativity – why not unleash the same potential at work?

Creativity has a sort of mystique about it. It is more often than not seen as the preserve of a gifted and privileged few. It bugs me in the marketing world where the word "creatives" is used to delineate a narrow subset of the people who work in that industry. In the BBC too there was a bizarre, and pervasive, distinction between creative jobs and everything else, as if creativity wasn't possible in every role. Isn't it creative if an accountant comes up with a game changing way of measuring things? Isn't it creative if a manager changes her interactions with her staff in a way that transforms their relationship?

Social tools afford the possibility to democratize creativity. On the Internet no one knows you are a dog. What does it matter who someone is, what they look like, or what their job title is if they come up with a stream of creative ideas or solutions to problems? Your possibilities for sharing your creative ideas are limitless, and the technology to bring them into form has never been so accessible. My teenage daughter produces informative, creative, and entertaining videos which she then shares on the web. Imagine if she applied that creativity to understanding your organization, sharing her knowledge, and making your business more effective? Or would you ban her from accessing YouTube at work?

Very often creativity comes out of mess and confusion. It is hard to be creative in a sterile, over organized environment. You need variety and stimulation, a connection with the real world, something that jolts you into seeing things differently, that lights the creative spark. This might be bouncing off other people, different people, people with views opposed to your own. It might be suddenly seeing things from a different perspective because of a blog post. It might be a post from someone who thought what they had said was ordinary and obvious to everyone but it wasn't to you – it was revelatory. It might come from seeing patterns in the views and behaviours of large numbers of people all expressing their views visibly for the first time. It might come from an unplanned comment in a mundane conversation. You need more of whatever kind of stimulus it takes to encourage creativity. You need this to be available to everyone. It doesn't have to remain the preserve of a creative clique, wearing trendy clothes, or being seen with the right people. It can be done quietly and unobtrusively online.

This is where online interaction within a business comes in. Spending time on an intranet forum allows you to rub shoulders with a melting pot of other staff and forces you to see other perspectives. There is also ample opportunity to pick up on ideas and run with them. With the right spark you can tap into the slightly obsessive focus online forums seem to generate. There is a playful willingness to hone in on a problem and solve it. Enough people spending five minutes in between "real" work to tinker with a problem online can achieve wonderful things. I have watched people attack engineering problems, business problems, and even personal problems online and arrive at effective solutions in a timescale hard to imagine any other way.

As an individual you need to get out of the victim mindset to be creative. You need to be willing to explore the possible, to be curious, to tinker. You need to have a playful attitude to problems and feel that solving them is within your power. This is not easy when you are sitting in an office on your own, or surrounded by people who adopt a victim mentality. With web tools you can seek out people who energize you, people who challenge you, people who stimulate you.

There is a real knack to allowing creativity to flourish. New ideas can be very fragile in the early days, not fully formed and at risk of being squashed. The trick for management is to notice when something is growing and then encourage it gently to flourish. If you react too early you can kill it. Having lots of managers pounce on you when you are chucking around daft ideas can be intimidating. If you try to systematize and replicate creative solutions too early, you take ownership away from those who thought of them. Managers have to learn to treat the online world as an ecology where ideas blossom and thrive but also where you need to be sensitive about how you tend them and the sort of environment they grow in.

You need to get used to having weeds too. You need to allow a thousand seeds to blossom and then have ways of selecting the best ones. In our past attempts to manage information and make it tidy, we have reduced the fertile, messy ground which is where real creativity and innovation happen. We need noisy robust exchanges to stimulate creative thinking. We can't expect people to conform to organizational culture and at the same time come up with wacky creative ideas. The usual solution to this is to have separate people who are charged with being creative, but this then ends up as a pretty unhealthy monoculture and loses the serendipitous connections so essential to true creativity.

People assume that our success inside the BBC with social tools was because we were a creative business. They think that we were different from them and their conservative organizational cultures. They think it was the trendy programme makers who embraced social media. This is totally wrong. In fact the creative people were the last to embrace social tools. Their status relied on an old culture and more exclusive approach to creativity and collaboration. It was in fact the "back room" folks who took to our social tools first. Groups like engineering, HR, finance. It was also mostly those who didn't already have a voice and wouldn't have been seen as creative. It satisfied an unmet need to engage and connect with each other and with problems that needed to be solved. Social tools tend to appeal to the disenfranchised and so it is those at the margins rather than the centre who tend to be drawn to them.

Stowe Boyd once used the word "edglings" to describe those of us attracted to using social tools. We are not at the centre or the top of things. In fact there is no centre or top, just edges. Different edges for different people. Networks of people at the edges of different things but who want to connect and form networks. People who have "being at the edge" in common with each other. People who don't need a middle to exist. Become comfortable with working things out as you go along, being prepared to break things. Keep moving, head for the high ground, and stay in touch.

There is something disruptive about creativity which is why many organizations are so keen to keep it in a box. There is also something inherently disruptive about social tools. The frequency and quality of interactions are no longer under management's control. People can bounce ideas off each other whenever and wherever they want. The effects can be unpredictable. My fantasy is a business where everyone blogs. Everyone thinks about what they are doing, and writes about what they are doing. From the top to the bottom, the edges to the middle. Everyone awake and bouncing off each other intellectually as they get more and more effective at whatever they do. This would be the ultimate in corporate creativity.

Things to remember:

- We tend to see creativity as the preserve of a privileged few.
- Everyone can be creative given the right circumstances.
- Creativity thrives in difference, mess, and connections. It dies in sterile environments. We need to take responsibility for creating the right environments both as organizations and as individuals.
- Managers need to be very sensitive to encouraging and nurturing creativity.
- Attempts at creativity are often fragile and easy to damage.
- The web is messy and unpredictable but unleashes all sorts of creativity.
- Social tools can unleash the same sort of creativity in the workplace. Creativity is disruptive by its very nature.

27

INNOVATION AND THE FORCES OF DISRUPTION

New ideas and new approaches are the lifeblood of business, but we bury them under process. We say we want innovation but at the same time are frightened of it. The path to innovation is shorter and safer when you use social media.

Innovation is another of those big words bandied around in organizations as if everyone agrees what it means and is comfortable with doing it. As ever, this is far from the case. The forces that make innovating difficult are considerable. The familiarity and comfort with current approaches, the "not invented here" challenge, and the fact that in order to agree to innovate you have to agree that there is something wrong with what you are currently doing. Innovation comes out of dissatisfaction with the status quo. If everything was perfect there would be no need for innovation.

But most organizations discourage dissent. You are not allowed to say that there is something wrong. Seeing things as being wrong marks you out as a troublemaker. Aren't those trying to change things inevitably going to be seen as causing trouble, even if they are trying to make things better? Having the courage to "tell it like it is" is the first step to being recognized as an innovator. You can see where things are wrong and can see a clear path to what will be right. Building consensus behind your vision and engaging others in bringing it about are the key skills of innovators.

Sadly innovation isn't so easy in most large organizations. It is seen as too important and too risky to leave to troublemakers. Instead it tends to be assigned to dedicated groups, set apart from the main day-to-day business. I was part of just such a group of innovation initiatives at the BBC, and while we tried as much as possible to root our work in the day-to-day, real world, it inevitably became marginalized. We were an overhead, off to the side somewhere, that people didn't have to take seriously. You can't do innovation by committee.

So where does the answer lie? Somewhere between the two extremes of troublemakers and committees. This is where social tools have a really important role to play. If, as I do, you believe in serendipity, the wisdom of crowds, and the fact that few people have all the answers, then networked tools are a good place to look for innovation.

If people facing challenges only ever meet the same people facing the same challenges then their ability to see the world differently is severely limited. If you add to this the fact that innovation is often not seen as part of their job, then a lot of people spend their days banging their heads against the same walls doing the same old things. If, on the other hand, you are able to describe your problem in an online forum, seen by the entire organization, then the chances of someone else who is facing the same problem – perhaps from a slightly different angle – coming to your aid increase. Also your post may be seen by someone from a different part of the organization, who is causing your problem. They may be unaware of this and once they know can simply agree to stop what they are doing or develop new processes to avoid your problem.

There are few people who have enough understanding to address the increasingly complex and varied challenges we face in the modern world. Having all of the bits of expertise at your disposal to come up with innovative solutions inevitably involves others. So innovation becomes a collaborative process. The way we have done collaboration until now is in committees or small groups but the web affords so many more effective ways of working together. Using wikis to work together developing new ideas is becoming commonplace. The ability to record collective thinking and then have that thinking remain flexible and visible helps the process of innovation. Things can keep moving and keep changing even when the idea has been delivered. In fact tools like wikis allow for continuous ongoing innovation. Why stop when you get to the first right answer? Why not keep innovating? Keep it going, keep tinkering, keep being curious.

Innovation comes about through being curious and tinkering. It is rarely the result, at least in the early stages, of structured thinking. Look at Google's oft quoted practice of requiring staff to spend a percentage of their time doing off the wall things. Several of Google's biggest and most successful initiatives have come out of this dedicated "play time". What is one man's time wasting is another man's world changing innovation.

As the Japanese showed with Kaisen, everyone has the potential to innovate whatever their job or level in the organization. If you distribute your innovation to the network, and do it incrementally, you open up all sorts of new opportunities and perspectives. You get away from the small group mindset and institutionalization that besets so many attempts at innovation. You also engender a robust "say what you think" culture that allows people to find fault with the status quo and start on the true path to innovation.

James Surowiecki, in his book *The Wisdom of Crowds*, described the ability of large groups of sufficiently diverse and dispersed individuals to deal with problems more effectively than small groups or experts a surprisingly high proportion of the time. His ideas are still debated and disagreed with in many circles, but at the very least the ability to have large groups of individuals – who needn't ever have met – addressing challenging problems is one way to drive innovation. Harnessing this principle through online tools allows for diversity and a high level of engagement from people who may not otherwise have the ability to work together.

The stereotypical idea of innovation is similar to creativity, the lone inventor or artist, musing alone and coming up with the world changing vision. It rarely happens like this. Creativity and innovation are inherently social processes. They come out of people operating in the world, seeing it differently, and having a reason to do something about it. They don't just happen – like so many of the things we have been looking at in this book. You can't just expect people to self-select around the need to innovate, though this can sometimes happen. You need to get good at describing challenges, approaching the right people, and setting up the circumstances for them to be able to work on innovative solutions together.

Things to remember:

■ Innovation is inherently disruptive as it entails finding fault with the status quo.

■ If you don't allow people to question how you currently do things you are unlikely to produce innovation.

■ Organizations often try to sanitize innovation – to do it by committee.

■ In complex situations finding ways to innovate is an increasingly social process.

■ Allowing people facing challenges to describe them online opens the door to others coming to their aid and finding solutions.

■ Accessing the wisdom of the crowds doesn't solve everything but it does allow you to focus more resources on coming up with new solutions.

■ You need to create the right culture and encourage connections to generate innovation online.

28

NO SUCH THING AS CONSCRIPTS

We need to make our organizations attractive to the smart people we want to employ. Nowadays most of them have grown up with the web and won't work for places that don't allow them to access the tools that they use to keep in touch with the networks that keep them smart.

Social media is going to increasingly affect recruitment. People who have grown up with the web and use social tools are frankly not going to work for organizations that won't let them continue to use these tools at work. In fact the very reason you employ smart people is often for the networks of other smart people which they are part of. Knowledge is less and less held in individuals and more and more in networks. If you sever the networks you devalue the individual. This is clearly the case where the expertise is in the web itself. Web developers have to maintain links with other web developers to keep up with their skills and knowledge. It is not in your interests to prevent them from doing so. I know of many instances where people have to wait until they get home to get full access to the web and reconnect with their knowledge base. It is ludicrous that they have to do so. This situation will increasingly arise with other skills and groups of experts. The web is about learning and sharing knowledge, and your bright young things will increasingly insist on being allowed to access it.

Another way in which the web will affect recruitment is in the increased transparency it brings. More and more people are talking about work and their employers on the web and you won't be able to stop them. It is not hard to search for a company name and unearth what are clearly groups of staff discussing their employers on Facebook or other networking sites. In the same way as we are able to find out more than ever before about the products we buy, through these online conversations we will be able to gain real insight into prospective employers.

Those employers will also be able to find out about us. Much has been made about recruitment teams searching Facebook and LinkedIn to find prospective candidates and the damage supposedly done by online indiscretions. In some ways this is an anachronistic attitude coming from people who don't themselves engage online. People are becoming much more robust and open in their online lives. Besides, what is so awful about these supposed indiscretions? Rather than worrying about photos of potential recruits drunk at parties, I would be more worried about people who appeared to have something to hide. In fact I would be less likely to employ someone who hadn't been indiscreet as a student!

When it comes to having our skills and knowledge valued, our power to create an online, personal brand has never been greater. This is more obviously a benefit for freelancers and the self-employed but even for those seeking full employment our online presence is increasingly important. Start building your network and credibility now. If you are claiming to be an expert and don't have any links to your name on Google you are going to have a hard time persuading recruiters of your value. Sharing your knowledge online and being seen to know your stuff is the best way to be attractive to prospective employers. This is possibly even more so internally where, if you have social tools inside the organization, your next opportunity will be all the more exciting if you have not only been seen to know what you are talking about but also willing and able to share it.

Internal recruitment for jobs could be done more interactively on the intranet. Being able to discuss jobs and share what they are really like and what you are really looking for could be a real time saver when it comes to interviews. HR issues aside, helping people understand what is expected of them will help them self-select better. There is also the prospect of widening the net if you use social tools. More people aware of the post you are seeking to fill, and talking about it online, will create more buzz than conventional approaches.

One of the reasons I got into social tools was when, as a line manager of editors, I was in the position of having to find work for staff. I had been given all sorts of expensive scheduling tools but could barely keep up with the networking and work finding that staff did for themselves. I remember thinking at the time, and we are talking about the late 90s here, that it would be great if each of my staff could have a web page on which they could lay out their skills and their availability. Prospective clients could then find the best match for them, work with the editors to find the best slot, and a lot of administrative overhead could be done away with overnight.

In terms of recruiting the best staff into your organizations, why not start building networks with potential employees before you recruit them? Maybe have a section of your internal forum accessible by the outside world where potential recruits could rub shoulders with existing staff. This would be rewarding for both groups and a great way to ensure not only that people know what to expect before you start the often lengthy and expensive recruitment process, but that when they do start working for you they can hit the ground running. You could engage with your internal networks in finding the right people. Why pay head hunters when you have possibly thousands of staff who have relationships and networks with people who might work for you? Engage your staff in finding new recruits and ask them to keep their eyes out for likely candidates when they are in their online communities. Once people leave you, why not allow them to stay connected as part of an alumni programme? They could be engaged in your recruitment activities even when they have left.

I was lucky enough to hear the management guru Peter Drucker speak in San Diego many years ago and during his presentation he said something that for me sums up the change in the relationship between employers and staff that we are only now truly seeing come to fruition. He said: "In a knowledge economy there are no such thing as conscripts – there are only volunteers. The problem is we have trained our managers to manage conscripts." We need to get better at making our organizations attractive to the smart people we need to make them successful. We need to acknowledge that people learn through their networks, and we need to help them maintain those networks as they make their way into our organizations.

Things to remember:

- Skilled people are increasingly part of networks. Rather than banning those networks use them to attract the best people.
- Younger generations have very different expectations of their employers and easy ubiquitous web access will be one of them.
- People will talk more online about your organization and what it is like to work there whether you encourage them to or not. Make sure they have something good to say.
- Build your personal brand online and be seen to be the most knowledgeable in your field.
- Engage your staff and their networks in the recruitment process and extend your conversations to new recruits – even before they arrive.
- We need to use our networks to attract and retain the smart staff we need.

29

HEADING INTO THE GREAT UNKNOWN

One of the challenges, and joys, of using social tools in business is that you don't know in advance what people are going to do with them or how they will develop. This is a challenge to some but liberating to others.

My team and I used to end our meetings, only half jokingly, with an American Marines saying which is "Keep moving, stay in touch, and head for the high ground." It seemed to make eminent sense in the world we found ourselves in with our social tools growing really quickly, not many people having done it before, and no rule books. If you think of it – having a rough and agreed idea where the high ground is, keeping moving and doing things rather than sitting around planning or strategizing, and keeping talking to each other while you do it all make eminent sense in modern, fast changing organizations. Contrast this with the conventional process for determining strategy which involves a small subset of the organization who, after an often lengthy process, deliver a finite, closed document that is, if anything, designed to close down communication rather than opening it up.

There is little doubt that some people feel more comfortable without a clear idea of where they are headed but it is becoming harder and harder to give them this with any confidence. Who could have predicted many of the recent financial disasters that have affected the economy, or the sudden demise of the communist bloc, or for that matter the impact of the web on the music and entertainment industries? In every large organization there are piles of expensively produced strategies gathering dust. They painted compelling pictures of futures that never happened.

It is a mistake to overplay change as an aspect of organizational life as if it was something new. Change has always happened. Perhaps arguably it now happens a bit faster and its results are less predictable. And yet some of the changes covered in this book are happening surprisingly slowly. We have had the Internet for thirty years, and the web for twenty, yet many people still don't know what the back button of their web browser does. We have had

LinkedIn in for six years and Twitter for five and yet they are still totally unfamiliar to many people. When asked recently how long I thought it would take for the full consequences of the web to be seen in our institutions and society at large I suggested fifty years. My answer was met with astonishment but I do think the changes we are talking about are that big: we are just at the start, and there will be a lot of resistance. This is all going to take longer than we think to fully work its way into society.

But we don't really know how or when. The rate of development of new tools is increasing all the time. The latest cool toy is arriving before the business world has accommodated the last. Much of this change is being driven by the consumer world rather than the business world and this is new. In the past work was the main place where people had access to computers. Now our computers at work are slower and more locked down than the technology most of us have at home.

So how do you get strategic when the world is this flexible? If you do have to have a formal strategy, why not write it on a wiki? Make it a living document which can grow and be adapted as circumstances change. How many businesses have got into trouble because their chief execs stuck to a particular strategic vision when their organization was screaming at them that it wasn't working? Why not allow the ebb and flow of the perceived future to be reflected in your strategy documents? By taking them less seriously you allow them to become more significant. By being strategically tactical you build ownership and consensus while creating your shared picture of where the high ground is and what it looks like.

The reassuring thing is that in some ways we are getting back to some simple essentials about human nature and how we relate to each other. Yes, the tools emerge at a frightening rate but most of them are enabling very human forms of interaction. In a way we are getting back to a more essential, pre-industrial, way of relating to one another and this gives us a degree of predictability and stability. Instead of tools that force us to see the world a particular way, like some of the large enterprise systems we have seen, social tools are there for us to make our own sense of the world and shape them to fit it. The good ones allow us to take ownership and to configure them to reflect our priorities and view of the world. They all rely on our desire to connect. David Weinberger once said that what held the Internet together wasn't Internet protocols but love. Love and the simple hyperlink are all we need to construct our own meaning and value in these new online worlds.

So how do you think ahead in this fast moving, self-organizing environment? You need to be strategically tactical. I believe it is possible to make a case to executive boards for adopting a tactical approach to new technology that lays out a general direction to the high ground, explains the tactic of keeping moving and staying in touch, and allows you to build reporting and decisions around this. You can explain that you have certain criteria and principles that you will apply in response to various situations and a process for applying them. You can also explain your tactical response to the flexible nature of the challenges. For instance if you are deploying any tools, either personally or in a business setting, make sure they import and export easily. You need to be able to up sticks and move to the next tool without too much pain and effort. This may come at the price of not doing all of the cool things a proprietary tool makes possible, but in the long run this is a price worth paying. This is also why it is worth sticking to the most common standards rather than getting painted into a corner by a particular vendor. I am not just talking big corporate stuff here – you try exporting the information you have built up in Facebook and let me know how you get on.

This interoperability of systems and standards is symptomatic of an ecology rather than a planned economy. We still try to run our corporations as planned economies. Kevin Carson, writing in his book *Organization Theory: A Libertarian Perspective*, says "The capitalist system of coordination by trade seems to be largely populated by indigestible lumps of socialism called corporations." We cling to central planning committees and quota mentalities and we bury ourselves under process. We need to get better at being strategically tactical and this will involve taking more of our staff with us as we work out new ways of working. If we can learn to manage more networked, fleet of foot, democratic, internal environments, then we increase our chances of achieving the flexibility we will need to succeed in the future.

Things to remember:

■ The world changes too quickly to persist with long-term strategies and centralized planning.

■ While change feels like it is happening fast, the underlying societal changes enabled by the web will take longer than we think.

■ Help people to learn to keep moving, stay in touch, and head for the high ground.

■ Build flexibility into your systems and lay out a strategy that embraces ongoing change rather than trying to predict a fixed future.

■ Make the case for being strategically tactical and spell out your approaches to responding to change and unpredictability.

30

BE STRATEGICALLY TACTICAL

How do you marry the fast moving and unpredictable world of social media with the corporate desire to strategize?

Strategizing tends to be done by a small group of very senior people backed up by hordes of outsiders from the big consultancy firms. They have a vested interest in convincing you and themselves that they are in control and know what is happening. This very conceit is madness. Strategy is one of those pompous grown-up words that no one questions. It confers on those who take part in strategizing almost mystical powers. Being allowed into that inner sanctum of those determining the future direction of the business is your average MBA's fantasy. But how often does anyone go back and see whether the strategy turned out to be right? How often does anyone do an ROI calculation of the costs of producing the strategy in the first place?

Let's face it – most strategies don't work. I don't just mean social media strategies – I mean all strategies. Given the time taken to recruit consultants, do the research, analyze the results, work out and negotiate the strategy, and then write and publish it, most of them are not worth the paper they are written on. The world has changed too fast and it now doesn't look like you thought it would. You've encased your expectations in the organizational concrete of an enterprise resource planning tool and the cracks are already starting to show. You have to start all over again . . . Don't get me wrong – the process of writing the strategy can be invaluable. The conversations that lead up to the creation of it, and those that take place while people discuss its rights and wrongs, relevance or lack of it, have immense value. But the chances of any corporate strategy reflecting either the world you want to live in or the one you inhabit now are very slim.

Yes, you need to have a big picture vision but why not make it bigger? Why not let everyone, particularly the youngsters who are going to inherit your strategy, get involved in writing it? Why not put your strategy on a wiki and allow people to update it as the world changes? Instead of casting it in stone, allow it to become a collectively owned, malleable vision of what the future might look like and how to get there. The scenario work pioneered at Shell by Arie de Geus and his team is much more what we are talking about here. Establishing collective stories about what might happen, where we might want to get, and how we might want to get there. Doing it online allows more people to take part in this process than ever before.

Shifting attitudes to strategy is not going to happen overnight. Too many people have too much invested in it, as I discovered myself at the BBC. Having read the book *Wisdom of Crowds* I had the wacky idea that we could use decision markets to decide the BBC's future strategy. Decision markets are where people buy shares in certain outcomes and the buying and selling of those shares gives you an indication of the collective view of what might work. We had a viewer site called Celebdaq which allowed people to buy and sell shares in celebrities and, depending on how much media coverage the celebrities got, people got more or less return on their investment. I had the temerity to suggest to senior management that as we already had this decision market engine I saw no reason why we couldn't turn this inside and allow BBC staff to buy and sell shares in various possible strategic directions. To tap into our collective intelligence and allow them to ensure that we had a better sense of a more realistic and achievable future. I got no reply.

So why do so many people start their social media activities with a strategy?! Because that is what you are expected to do! How can you start anything in business without a clear strategy? Well with social media, frankly you would be mad to. You really don't know before you put the tools in, and people start using them, how things are going to turn out. Yes you can have a rough idea of where you are headed and what you want to get out of all of your activity, but at all costs avoid taking this too seriously because it is almost certainly not where you will end up. Remember the US Marines saying "Keep moving, stay in touch, and head for the high ground" and I reckon that is about as good as it gets with social media strategy. Or any other strategy for that matter.

Why am I so confident about this? Because the whole point of adopting social media in an organization is to allow the messy, serendipitous, opportunistic "real" world to finally take its place alongside the more formal, structured, managed "fantasy" many organizations are stuck in. If you go down the road of deploying these disruptive web tools it will be to mitigate the effects of a rigid corporate environment backed up by rigid IT. You will be doing it to let the organism that is the organization breathe. Don't stifle it with strategy.

Things to remember:

■ Strategizing is an expensive and time consuming process, usually carried out by a small subset of the organization, which rarely works.

■ The whole point of deploying social tools is to enable the organic, networked world to take its place alongside the more structured, formal one. Don't kill this with a rigid strategy.

■ By their very nature it is hard to predict where your use of social tools will take you. Decide to be strategically tactical.

■ The main benefit of writing a strategy is in the process of writing it. Why not enable more people to be part of this process?

■ The corporate approach to strategy is not going to change overnight. Start small and aim high!

31

BACK TO FRONT ROI

Quantifying the return on investment on anything to do with increasing intangible assets has always been difficult and social media is no different. But what if we are asking the question back to front?

Return On Investment – another of those grown-up phrases that gets bandied about and which can send a chill down your spine. It is taken for granted that being able to quantify a return on investment is an essential part of justifying any new initiative you are trying to get off the ground. It would be naïve to suggest that it is a pointless exercise. For projects with predictable and quantifiable outcomes it is useful to have a sense – before you embark on them – of what you are going to get as a return for your investment of time and effort. The problem is that it has been assumed that you can apply this sort of thinking to any and all initiatives.

But in some cases you don't know exactly what the outcomes are going to be and you will struggle to quantify realistically the results of your actions. In fact it is arguably the case that most of the really world changing developments in technology and business would find it hard to produce a realistic estimate of return on investment. Remember the days when people laughed at Google for their lack of a business model and ridiculed their apparent naïvety in giving services away for nothing. And here they are now, one of the biggest revenue earning advertising platforms in the world. People similarly mocked Facebook and Twitter for not having business models in advance, but both of them have achieved enormous market valuations on the strength of the scale and ubiquity of their services – even though it is still not totally clear how they are going to monetize what they do.

All of these concerns will be equally true of your attempts to get social media accepted in the workplace. There will be no shortage of people asking you to justify the ROI of corporate blogging or staff forums, and it is not always easy to give them an answer. In fact when I was doing this work at the BBC I tried my hardest to avoid people who asked that kind of question for as long as I could. It was easier in those days, and I was able to decide to ask for forgiveness rather than permission. Especially if you are using low cost technologies, as I advocate throughout this book, it is possible to get a lot done without having to ask for too much money or having to ask permission from too many people. If you grow your activities incrementally – and avoid large, expensive, initiatives – you too will hopefully manage to avoid a lot of the people who are inclined to ask the ROI question. In fact I once offered a Scotsman's tip on ROI – keep the "I" really small and no one will give you hassle about the "R"!

This isn't to say that what you are doing isn't measurable. In fact, paradoxically, it is much more measurable than much of our current business activity. All online activity is recorded and can be very accurately reported on. You can see how much time people are spending using your tools, how much their contributions are used by others, and how much value they are creating.

In anticipation of being asked to justify our work I used to watch all of our social tools and look for those times when either an opportunity had been gained that would otherwise have been lost, or where a risk had been averted or minimized thanks to online conversations. I would then approach the people involved and ask them to put a rough figure on how much they had gained, or saved, thanks to the online conversations. I collected a pack of these stories to keep in my back pocket ready to produce them if and when anyone asked the ROI question. It rarely happened. In part this was because we knew that if we got our tools useful enough, to enough people, fast enough, then by the time those inclined to ask the ROI question thought of doing so, the benefits would be such a no-brainer that no one would ask it.

As more and more people begin to use social tools at work, the question is not so much *whether* others will follow them as *when*. There may be businesses which never deploy social tools but they will increasingly be the exception rather than the rule. Given this, I am becoming more robust about the ROI question and turning it back on those who ask it. What is the ROI of the way we do things now? We rarely question the ROI of the many meetings where people in business spend their days. We don't question the ROI of all the time spent writing and formatting documents that few people ever read. I look at the large open plan offices, common in many organizations, and see all these people staring at computer screens, often using only a small percentage of what the technology is capable of, and in the process not talking to each other. What's the ROI of that?

As a final resort, consider turning the ROI question on its head. Given that it appears inevitable that the web and social tools are going to become an even more significant part of how we do things, instead of asking me to justify the ROI of encouraging this process – justify to me the ROI of stopping it. What is the financial benefit of continuing to do things in inefficient ways when there are more effective alternatives available? Where is the competitive advantage in preventing staff from using these tools to build and maintain the networks that develop their knowledge and their ability to get things done? Where is the competitive advantage in allowing your competitors to embrace these changes before you do and potentially re-inventing the industry you are so rigidly clinging to?

Things to remember:

- Applying return on investment thinking to intangible assets has always been difficult.
- Most world changing initiatives would never have got off the ground if required to guarantee an upfront return on investment.
- We don't question the ROI on the many inefficient ways we currently do things.
- What is the ROI of preventing social media from happening?

32

THE PRICE OF POMPOSITY

By adopting a disapproving tone in business we inhibit free exchange of ideas and innovation. Our concern for status weakens our ability to lead. Online conversations force us to lighten up.

There is such a strong culture of disapproval in business. Of needing to stay on top of people for fear that if you don't they will run riot. This infects the language we use and the attitudes we adopt as managers. "Who do you think you are to say that?" "I didn't get where I am today . . . " "You're here to work not to have fun." It is remarkable how many managers have forgotten how to speak normally. It is almost a defensive thing. We hide behind language that is cold and dispassionate and use concepts that are abstract and clinical. All in an almost explicit attempt to hide the messiness of being human.

I can remember in my first managerial job, as a line manager of fifty staff, being terrified at the prospect of "being responsible" for all of these people. In fact that is a telling phrase in itself – how could I be seen as responsible for fifty grown-ups, many of whom knew more than me about the business we were in? Initially I let the fear get to me and I started wearing a tie and talking funny. I retreated into management speak to distance myself from those I was "responsible for" and wore my uniform like armour. When faced with dealing with redundancies and having to talk to someone old enough to be my father who broke down in tears in front of me, the temptation was to recoil, to run away and hide behind my tie and my language. Thankfully I managed to resist that temptation and to stay there, stay part of the conversation, and continue to treat him as a fellow human being rather than just a member of staff. Thankfully I realized what was happening to me and I stepped back from the brink. Many, if not most, don't and descend that slippery slope into pompous management speak.

Pomposity doesn't work on the web. Plain speaking conversations between people are what works. But many businesses struggle with the different approach required online and some of those in positions of authority maintain their pompous tone. This pomposity can often manifest itself in disapproval and a rejection of the web as a whole. "It's all rubbish", "It's all just people expressing their opinions", "It is all just people wasting their time." This is such a common reaction from those in business and it is invariably delivered in a condescending tone. "The level of people I work with are far too busy to worry about what the world and his dog had for breakfast." But how do they think such disapproval makes those involved on the web feel? Do they think it makes them look clever? Do they think we didn't realize what a waste of time the web was until they helpfully pointed it out? In fact pomposity harms those who indulge in it online. They stick out like sore thumbs. They become the focus of ridicule, and will be avoided at all costs and cut out of networks. The ultimate irony is using Twitter to pompously tell those who use Twitter how useless Twitter is! The status which made those who act in this way feel pompous in the first place will begin to diminish as they are less and less included in the latest and most interesting conversations. Eventually they will become isolated and powerless.

Very often people are pompous because they are nervous. It is a form of protection. Increasingly they are aware that something significant is happening online and their lack of competence in it scares them. They believe they see values changing and the old familiar world of command and control and job titles weakening. This is where we should be gentle with them, forgive them their disapproval, and try to help them understand.

There is a high price to be paid for all of this disapproval – both by those who disapprove and those who are disapproved of. It doesn't allow those who indulge in it to engage with people or become vulnerable enough to allow real connection to happen. If you react with cool dispassion or even disapproval when someone comes to you with their heartfelt opinion or newly formed and fragile idea, then you do them harm. You exercise violence in the pursuit of status and also decrease efficiency. You risk becoming less than you can be both as an individual and as an organization.

The feeling of staying with the conversation, of being authentic and having nowhere to hide, while important face to face is even greater online. In fact I suspect it is one of the things that makes people wary of online conversations – the openness and the accountability can be challenging. It is less easy to hide online in some ways than it is face to face. The medium calls for directness and use of plain language rather than florid management speak. This direct, first person language can be frightening to use. Watch how kids write. It is totally different. Set aside their poor spelling and grammar and watch them convey ideas with ruthless efficiency. They write in a totally different tone. They write as equals. They write to earn attention rather than to wield authority. They write for each other, not to hear the sound of their own voice. Their own voice is a group voice not an exclusive voice. You have to say what you think plainly and simply. You can't hide behind your status or your pomposity. In fact being remote and pompous will severely inhibit your attempts at effective communication on the web.

So the answer is to help those who are disapproving or pompous in reaction to what is happening on the web. Don't dismiss their reactions or sneer at them but make it easier for them to relax and say what they think. Show them the ropes and hold their hands rather than ridicule them as they discover for themselves the fast changing world they have felt excluded from. We have to help them lighten up and not take themselves or their work so seriously. In a way the web is like going back to a less inhibited childhood or perhaps teenage years. The ability to play at being different types of people and not having to adhere to a possibly uncomfortable role. The ability to be yourself rather than the role you have found yourself becoming. Loosen the bonds and relax into more engaging and effective conversations. Get over your self-importance. Write to entice rather than to berate or lecture, offer up ideas rather than force them down people's throats.

> **Things to remember:**
>
> ■ We hide behind cold business language as a protection against the messiness and unpredictability of being human.
>
> ■ Pomposity sticks out like a sore thumb online where it is in stark contrast to the prevailing informality and light tone.
>
> ■ People are often pompous or disapproving of things they are afraid of. Help them to be less afraid.
>
> ■ Disapproval and pomposity get in the way of genuine communication and prevent us from reaching our full potential.
>
> ■ Lose any sense of self-importance you have and write to entice and interest people – not to lecture them.

33

MANAGING THE MESS

People fear the apparent messiness of online environments but sometimes making things more organized makes them harder to find. One person's sensible taxonomy is another person's gobbledegook. How do you get the best of the formal and informal ways we have of organizing information?

We expend a lot of effort in business tidying up. Organizations are about being organized. Being messy is seen as being inefficient. Management is about maintaining order, often at any cost. But what would happen if we let things go wild? What would happen if we let people build their own spaces in their own way? If we didn't insist on a uniform, corporate style for our intranet would people find it a more attractive place to spend time and would we find it easier to navigate? There is no consistent style or navigation for the Internet, and yes, this can be frustrating at times, but billions of people spend lots of time in there – unlike your average intranet.

It occurred to me while we were growing our forum at the BBC that what we were doing was encouraging the growth of the equivalent of old villages. Pretty places where no one predetermined the architectural style or insisted that all the roofs looked the same, but places that work. They work as places to live and people know how to get around them. There are well worn paths between the church and the pub and you always know where you are. If you bump into someone else you are happy to stand around on a street corner chatting. They are places you want to hang around in. By contrast most intranets and IT systems are like new towns. Efficient on the face of it, with their designed paths and interchanges, but bewildering to navigate. There are plenty of road signs but you don't know what they mean, and if you get lost you don't really fancy standing around on a street corner waiting for a stranger.

When we started our forum we kept things deliberately very simple with little or no structure. There were only two folders, one for asking questions and the other for more general discussions. The structure grew out of people's activity. We navigated by linking to things and patterns emerged out of what got linked to most. As these patterns repeated we added folders to cover those topics.

But for some this organic approach was too homogenous, too messy – they wanted more structure. So we spent a lot of money building a new system with department and function based forums and a hierarchical structure, all nicely colour coded. Those who didn't use the platform much, but had demanded the changes, were very happy. The rest of us felt we had lost something and regretted what we had done. My small victory was to insist that the general "water cooler" space be kept easily accessible at the top of the front page and this ended up being where most people spent most of their time. It was a small victory and some of the soul of our shared space had been lost in an attempt to make it more organized.

This desire to organize extends into formal taxonomies, the attempt to make things more findable by consistently labelling them. There is a long and respected discipline of information management which I don't mean to belittle and which does perform a valuable function – but is it enough? I think we all at times attempt to organize our own hard drives by putting documents into labelled, nested folders. We can spend hours doing this but how often is this how we actually find things? Don't we have our own con-textual overlay of the neat folder structure? Don't we set off trying to remember where we put things rather than applying our own discipline? Don't we find things online through search, memory, association, and asking others? Remember Yahoo and its index of the web? Even if we have done a good job of establishing our information hierarchy, the world keeps changing anyway. It keeps evolving and moving on, so any attempt at manifesting this in a manmade structure is going to be a laborious, ongoing process.

Dave Snowden once said "You can't manage knowledge but you can create a knowledge ecology." I took this to mean building a variety of tools and platforms for people to write and share what they knew. I didn't want to build an over designed, over engineered system. Instead of buying or building single large systems you can encourage the growth of a variety of information tools and practices which allow people to grow their resources and to establish more organic ways of navigating them. If everything conforms to web standards people simply link to the right information wherever, and however, it is stored.

The skills to develop this ecology, or build the old village, are different from the ones needed when you were building the knowledge equivalent of massive structured buildings or cities. Take for example a wiki. Wikis encourage new information and growth but can get messy quickly. Rather than controlling the messiness, to begin with you are more interested in encouraging growth. You can always trim afterwards, and indeed the phrase gardening is often used to describe the process of tidying up a wiki once it has been in use for a while. Once you have done some tidying up, and the information in the wiki is consolidated enough to be reliable, you can export it to your more formal, and more managed, information tools.

Formal or informal, structured or unstructured? Does one approach work better than the other? It's not really a case of either/or. You want both. Both work in their own ways and having both in combination is very powerful. If you encourage an ecology to grow around your more formal information systems, then people can use these contextual spaces to navigate their way to what is relevant in the structured space. You need to have people with the right skills and outlook responsible for the two environments. Don't have people trying to make your social spaces too tidy and don't throw out the rule book when it comes to your formal data stores. We have an imbalance at the moment because most business information systems are formal and managed to be as tidy as possible. The people responsible for them have been brought up to see the world a certain way. One of the greatest challenges of getting social tools adopted in business is asking these people to allow a little bit of messiness around the edges, to encourage the growth of natural spaces in the centre of their new towns. It will take a while for them to get used to it but we will end up with more pleasant and effective places to work in.

Things to remember:

- Sometimes our attempts to organize our information make it harder to find.
- What looks messy to one person can appear easily navigable to another.
- We have been so keen to reduce mess in business that we have built sterile information environments where people don't spend much time.
- Combine social spaces and information tools with your more formal approaches to get the best of both worlds.
- Create a "knowledge ecology" and employ some good gardeners!

34

WE NEED MORE RUBBISH

We put a lot of effort into making our organizations organized, but maybe we have lost something in the process. Maybe in our attempts to improve our signal to noise ratio we have lost the signal.

A lot of the time and effort of management goes into tidying up and keeping things orderly. Reducing inefficient waste and unnecessary effort has been the focus of generations of managers. Arguably more of them are comfortable with this role than with more growth orientated leadership roles. Containment rather than promotion. Well it is going to be these managers' worst nightmare when I now suggest that we want more rubbish. As if there wasn't enough rubbish on the Internet I am saying we want more of it and, worse still – we need more of it at work. If staff don't talk enough rubbish, I am saying we should encourage them to talk more of it. Why? Signal to noise.

In our attempts to tidy up our information spaces and our business conversations, our efforts to reduce the noise have also meant that we have hidden the signals. The weak signals that can be so crucial in avoiding risks and making the most of opportunities. If we build a tidy new town rather than a messy old village we risk having a very clean, sanitized environment where nothing interesting happens. We all know businesses with "knowledge repositories" full of tidy but uninteresting documents rather than interesting lively spaces where information grows and flourishes. Also if we preempt what we deem valuable and allow one group to exercise disapproval of others having their say and dismiss it as rubbish, then we will end up with tidy but unhealthy monocultures. If it is really rubbish then we just ignore it and move on, but if we cause every daft idea to shrivel up even before it has reached our lips then we will miss so many wonderful opportunities.

Don't be too quick to dismiss someone as talking rubbish. One person's rubbish could be another person's gold dust. It costs little to let them express themselves and indeed to keep a record of what they are saying. If they really talk rubbish consistently then it proves they don't know what they are talking about and you get to know that and do something about it. If they don't then maybe some of their rubbish may have a value you just haven't perceived yet. Some people get very squeamish around what they perceive as rubbish. It produces a very strongly adverse reaction in them. The strong reaction from people who don't understand Twitter is an example of this. The strength of feeling is worth exploring. Why such resistance? Why the feeling of revulsion? What underlying truth has this little bit of rubbish revealed?

There are two types of rubbish. The kind that provokes a reaction while it is happening, and old stuff that doesn't appear to have longer term value. Current rubbish can be enervating but you learn to ignore it if you understand that with it comes the possibility of unforeseen value. Old rubbish, on the other hand, left to its own devices often increases in value – it ferments and re-constitutes itself into valuable nutrients. Don't be in too much of a hurry to tidy up after things have moved on. Don't archive online conversations too soon – keep them accessible. Keep your information in a place where it can be reused and pointed to in more current conversations.

It is common in online forums for things that had appeared moribund to suddenly spring to life again because what had appeared to be dead and valueless information suddenly had currency and significance again. If you have tidied it all up and locked it away, this recycling can't happen. Corporations have a legal responsibility to maintain copies of their rubbish but they often do so in inaccessible places. Leave your rubbish lying around so that people can scavenge and pick it up. Storage is cheap. Collect your rubbish. Recycle it. Use it for other and unintended purposes. The whole idea of the long tail is based on the potential of what some would have seen as rubbish and noise. Amazon have built a business on making the long tail accessible. It costs them so little to do so and someone somewhere perceives value in what would otherwise be seen as rubbish. What is your organization's information long tail? What is the weak signal, peripheral stuff that if collected and interpreted differently could have real and lasting value? Are you confining yourself to the equivalent of best sellers and missing out on the quirky but useful things that can make a big difference?

Finding the good stuff is one of the functions of bloggers. Information rag and bone men who curate the weak signal and the long tail. Seeing patterns in the small, the marginal, the messy. This is where those with nerdy curiosity and a good eye can find real value in what others have discarded or not noticed. Boosting these weak signals so that they last long enough to travel long distances takes effort and care. Finding them, recording them, and nurturing them are important skills. Separating signal in a dynamic way from the noise. Curation is becoming one of the most valued skills on the Internet. Pulling together the good stuff. Separating the signal from the noise and boosting it. We will all have to develop these skills. Recycling has become a way of life for many of us. Why not apply this to information and knowledge? Keep your knowledge equivalent of potato peelings and use them to generate compost. Pile more rubbish on the bits of the garden you want to grow and employ gardeners who tend and care for your baby shoots rather than disinfecting your information spaces.

Things to remember:

- In our attempts to tidy our information and communication we risk losing the signal along with the noise.
- It is often in weak signals that we discover opportunities or are alerted to threats.
- In order to encourage more signal you also need to tolerate more noise.
- Keep old information accessible and discoverable. Amazon make a living out of this long tail of information – you can too.
- Encourage curation of your information by those with an eye for the quirky and interesting.
- Allow those with information green fingers to encourage information to flourish.

35

LINES IN THE SAND

There are a lot of policies being written about social media by people who have little experience of using the tools and whose main interest is to control the use of them. Write enabling rules instead. Writing rules that make it easier to do the right thing is the way to influence behaviour.

Rules. To have them or not to have them? I worry when corporations start their social media efforts with writing rules – often before they really understand what they are writing rules about. It is a bit like writing the manual for running before you have learned to walk. I guess it stems from the paranoia that exists about what will happen when you give staff the ability to speak for themselves in a public forum. Without rules won't they run amuck? But isn't it funny how it's always someone else who will misbehave? Look at email. Everyone rants about email but it is always other people's misbehaviour that is identified as the problem. Rule making is often a projection of one group's worst expectations onto other people. The chaos they anticipate without rules very, very rarely comes to pass. Your biggest problem is not that people are going to behave like idiots but that they get so scared of breaking a rule that they end up saying nothing!

If you are going to have rules make sure they are enabling rules. Avoid language like "policy" or "rules" and prefer instead the sort of language used by the US Military with their *Social Media Handbook*. Make sure that your handbook is written for "us" and not for "you" – certainly not for "them". It is there to help everyone get clear about what is OK to do and what is not. Why not involve those who are going to be affected by your guidelines in the writing of them?

When we decided we needed some social platform guidelines at the BBC we got everyone involved. We had a corporate yellow pages tool at the time and we used this to discover the 400 people who worked for the BBC and admitted to having a blog. We approached those people and asked them what sort of things they were concerned about in terms of their use of social tools, though this was way before they were even called that, and what they thought we should include in the guidelines. We then wrote a draft document and stuck it on our wiki. We asked our group of bloggers to come in and improve what we had written, and then sat back and watched as they refined it, corrected it, and altered it until they were happy and the rate of changes eventually slowed down. At this point we realized that we had our guidelines which, as far as I know, with a few updates, still stand to this day.

Think of your goal more as developing a constitution than writing a rule book. A way for people to recognize in a formal way what works and what doesn't. To acknowledge responsibility publicly and to have some clear lines drawn in the sand just in case anything ever goes wrong. Get as many people as possible involved in the process of writing the guidelines. If you get this right, when you come to make them live everyone will just line up neatly behind them and be comfortable with them.

See your work as constantly evolving. Use your forums to have discussions about best practice and how to deal with new situations. As these begin to look consistent, write them up as FAQs. Over time as these continue to be relevant, move them to a wiki so that you can keep editing them. Clearly you will have to have a legal version hidden away in a knowledge coffin somewhere but don't make this your only version and certainly not your day-to-day working one. Have a process that everyone understands for differentiating between the working hypothesis and the cast in stone legal version. The world is moving ever faster and the world of online conversations even more so. It is a good idea not to cast your guidelines in stone but to keep them as a continuing working consensus.

Be very aware that those who perceive the greatest need for guidelines are invariably those who most resist social tools in the first place. Gatekeepers, those charged with maintaining the status quo, love rules and they will find plenty of reasons to constrain your efforts to establish new ways of working with what will no doubt sound like legitimate concerns. There will be enough barriers and constraints thrown in your path without making this another one. You may well have to be robust in your defence of this consultative process that you are adopting for generating your rules but trust me – in the long run it will be worth it.

If the prospect of this "grow your own" approach to guidelines seems daunting, or you are under pressure to come up with some rules before you are even allowed to start, don't worry. There are other ways of approaching the problem. You could go and look at other people's policies and there are now hundreds of these available on the Internet, including the one we did at the BBC. You can pick and mix from other people's policies and get an idea of what works. At least this will get you far enough to be able to get started. You could even get someone else to write your guidelines for you, but both of these options are far from ideal. You need to own this document. It needs to be relevant and alive. There is no point trying to steer what is meant to be a lively collaborative environment with a dry, boring straightjacket written by control freaks.

Getting a relevant and workable set of guidelines is part of growing up in social media. You don't want to grow up before you have to but you don't want to stay an unruly teenager all of your life. See it as an opportunity to showcase what can be done with social tools. If you can make this an efficient and effective process it sends a strong signal to others that social media isn't just for idle chatting but can be used for grown-up stuff too. Wherever you end up storing your document, make sure it is linkable and quotable – it has to become lively and relevant enough that people feel comfortable quoting it in their day-to-day use of the tools rather than something that is only dragged out of the cupboard when someone is going to get slapped for doing something wrong.

If you get it right your policy can become a model for things to come. Not just in terms of the process of writing it but also in what it says about the governance of the business. If this collaborative approach to rule writing works, why not apply it to other aspects of work? Getting people involved in the processes that govern their work is a great way of increasing their sense of ownership and responsibility. American Traci Fenton from World Blu runs an annual competition to recognize "the world's most democratic organization". Many people balk at the idea, but as we saw at the start of the book democracy is deemed – by most of us in the Western world at least – to be the best way to run nation states – so why shouldn't it work for your organization? This set of guidelines could be your first step on the way to winning the prize.

Things to remember:

- Don't start with rules. Learn to use your tools, and see how people make them work before you cast too much in stone.
- Aim to have rules and guidelines that enable the use of your platforms rather than inhibit them.
- Involve those who use the tools in the writing of your handbook and make the rules theirs.
- If this works well, why not apply collective policy making to other aspects of your organization?

36

SMALL PIECES
LOOSELY JOINED

The Internet is the largest manmade thing ever, but it is not owned or managed by anyone. Why not tap into this power and apply the same principles at work?

What has made the web successful is the way it allows lots of small things to work together, without overt or centralized management, to achieve wonderful things. On the face of it, it shouldn't work – and yet it does. In fact if you were to try to "run" the web using conventional management approaches it would grind to a halt. At its core there are certain things – standards – that, unless rigidly adhered to, would make the whole thing stop working, but so long as you stick with these standards there is enormous flexibility in what you can do.

How would it be if you took the principles that appear to have allowed the web to work and applied them more widely – in general management for instance? What if you had a few, very rigid, but really thought out rules at the core of your processes – and then gave people lots of flexibility as to how they applied these rules? Instead we try to control everything, and the more complex the environment the more rules we feel we need. Dave Snowden once said "If you want to try to manage a complex environment with complex tools, you end up with a mess. The only way to manage complex environments is with a small number of simple, universally understood rules."

What does this mean in reality? Well, take corporate social media policies. Many of them try to cover every eventuality and give precise direction on what to do in a wide range of very different circumstances. Like so many corporate policies they become almost unworkable, and are clearly there not so much to make it easier to do the right thing as to cover the organizations' backsides when things go wrong. Doc Searls once said "There are only two rules to corporate blogging. Rule No. 1 – don't be stupid. Rule No. 2 – if you are going to be stupid be prepared to pay the price." Now arguably there are shades of grey as to what stupid is, and I have described elsewhere ways of achieving a consensus on what doing the right thing looks like using the tools themselves. However, if you haven't distilled the essence of your rules to something simple enough to remember, and universal enough to apply flexibly, then you might as well not have written them.

The other shift required to achieve small pieces loosely joined as a way of working is the way we approach IT projects. There are so many examples of centralized, corporation-wide, IT projects that end up going over budget, over time, and failing to deliver. In fact the cynic in me might argue the case that this is true more often than not. Some of us were chatting online recently about the succession of massive IT project failures in the NHS and were exploring how we might have done it instead. As a first step we'd have got some hackers and geeks together with some people working in a local hospital and knocked up something simple and cheap. We would have then put this to use, being open about it being a best endeavours beta, and see how things went. We'd watch what worked and what didn't, go through lots of fast iterations, and, once we had something that seemed to be making things easier or more effective, we would invite people from another department to take a look. If they liked what they saw we'd offer it to them, maybe morphing it a bit to meet their needs. We'd build just enough hooks into the original so that the tools could connect to each other, and then repeat the process.

Once we had covered the various needs of the first local hospital we'd invite similar folks from a nearby hospital over to take a look and start the process again. This kind of low level, almost amateur, noodling with minimal resources and deliberately low expectations could arguably get a lot further, a lot quicker, for a lot less money than some of the classically run projects that we have seen fail so often. And the thing is that even if it doesn't work you haven't lost much and will have learned a lot. Shrug your shoulders and start again. No big deal – just small pieces loosely joined.

The thing is that this approach doesn't fit easily with the macho, big scope, big budget, "big willy" thinking that has become so prevalent in IT. It will take a different mindset and a different culture. In fact I was talking to some female IT managers recently and it became clear that their approach is very different from their male colleagues and much more webby than conventional IT. Hopefully as more people get more pragmatic about their IT, and it is seen less as the preserve of a small number of male specialists and more the interest and responsibility of the whole organization, we will begin to see real progress.

Keeping the small pieces loosely joined doesn't just happen though. You can't expect it all to hang together without effort. But it is a different kind of effort. It takes a lot of observation, a lot of listening, a lot of communication. Indeed skills stereotypically seen as the preserve of women. It is also more fun and more creative. When there is less at stake you can afford to be more creative. You can afford to be patient. If things don't work at first you wait. If they don't work in one place you let other people use them. You take an ecological approach rather than a machine approach. This allows you to keep adding small pieces or taking some out if you don't need them.

Someone once described me as an "intrapreneur", an entrepreneur operating inside a large organization. It is possible to adopt the ways of the web with this entrepreneurial spirit and help large organizations become more agile and flexible. Help them become more like the high churn, highly flexible world of the web and consumer technology than the traditional world of corporate IT. With this combination of simple rules and a tactical, perpetual beta approach to technology it is possible to turn your large enterprise into small pieces loosely joined.

Things to remember:

- The web is the largest manmade thing the world has ever seen but it is not owned or managed.
- It hangs together due to a small number of strictly adhered to rules or principles.
- You can adopt the ways of the web inside large organizations.
- Have a few simple but really strictly adhered to rules rather than trying to micromanage complexity.
- Adopt an exploratory, perpetual beta attitude to technology and you will get further, faster and more cheaply than most conventional large scale IT projects.
- Become an intrapreneur and help your organization become more agile and flexible.

37

UNLEASH YOUR
TROJAN MICE

Instead of having expensive tools or large scale change initiatives, have lots of small ones. Small things that don't require a lot of budget or permission from too many people but that will work away together to achieve significant benefits.

Conventional initiatives are like the more familiar Trojan Horse. Big, lumbering, slow moving. It takes a lot of people to move it and it is very hard to get it to change direction without a lot of effort. It is also very slow moving and risks not making it to its destination at all. As we deployed low cost small tools and kicked off little initiatives at the BBC we began to describe our approach as deploying Trojan Mice, a metaphor borrowed from the British consultant Peter Fryer. Set up small, unobtrusive, inexpensive, and autonomous tools and practices, set them running, and cajole and nudge them until they begin to work out where to go and why. In contrast to the Trojan Horse, Trojan Mice won't allow you to steer them precisely. They run around really fast with no apparent destination in mind. They don't require direction and work not only without external control but to some extent independently of each other. But they do know where the food is! They can together work out what works and keep doing it until they succeed. They can also represent a significant challenge and are very difficult to stop.

An incremental approach seems ideally suited to deploying social tools at work. People need to buy into them and engage with them gradually. Large scale initiatives tend not to work so well and we are in a period of such fast development that it is difficult to predict a future technology environment with any confidence. It is easy to go numb in the face of the question "what are we going to do with all this social media stuff and what are we going to get in return for our efforts?" We are used to feeling that we have to lay out our futures, write strategies and confidently predict a sequence of events that, when followed, will lead to a certain outcome. We could argue whether, even in more conventional worlds, the future rarely ends up looking like our strategies, but the unpredictable world of social tools makes this even harder to do. You are not always sure which tools are going to work or what people are going to do with them. The whole nature of it is that people take ownership and responsibility for the outcomes, so how do you lay out a future direction if you are not sure what they are going to do?

When we were setting off at the BBC I wasted a lot of time writing strategy papers for John Birt, the Director General at the time. I spent a lot of time and energy painting pictures of the perfect world I was going to create for the BBC but kept bouncing off him because they were not pictures of his perfect world and I had no real conviction that we were going to end up where I said we would. In fact I felt kind of deceitful for even pretending that I knew where things were headed and had any confidence that we would get there.

So instead of strategizing we started building networks. We started building tools. I got on much better when I decided to ask for forgiveness rather than permission and started to just do things. Not to over plan and try to do things in the abstract but to get concrete and actually build tools and make them work. We bought very cheap forum software, put it on our own server, started using it ourselves, showed it to a few others and the next thing you know, well six years later to be fair, we have 25,000 BBC staff users.

So what does this mean in practical terms? It means allowing people to set up their own initiatives using your tools and establish their own groups no matter how small. Watch what they are doing and see what works. Keep telling stories about what is happening and share what is working with people who you think it would benefit. Encourage them to copy what is working and to develop it further in their own spaces. Work together to determine some simple operating principles for what works and proactively share these. Build networks of people running the networks and harness their collective energy and learning.

This approach applies not just to people but also to technology. We used four or five free or cheap tools and adapted them to our needs. Rather than buy one big elaborately constructed, overarching enterprise system, buy lots of little inexpensive things that will join up loosely. Use things from the web, copy and reuse code, use open source tools with thriving communities and adapt them for your own use. Rather than limiting and controlling the use of tools, allow them to grow and flourish. So long as you are spending small amounts of money, you can even allow more than one tool to kick off at the same time and allow the fitter one to survive.

This is the way the Internet works – small things loosely joined. Have a low cost, throw away approach to tools that people take ownership of and help these to join up into effective collections of tools and behaviours over time, using standards and protocols rather than controls. Another benefit of the idea of Trojan Mice is that they are small. They don't have to be very expensive or take a lot of investment. You are not risking a lot if you lose the odd mouse. You can afford to have a few failures and this allows you to be braver and try more adventurous things.

So how do you manage a world of Trojan Mice? How do you make it more likely for Trojan Mice to get where you want them to? Do you create runs for them, making it easy to go in the right direction and blocking off alternative routes? How do you get them to achieve a productive outcome for their efforts? How do you make them productive and not destructive? This goes back to being strategically tactical and heading for the high ground. You have to spend a lot of energy explaining where you want to get to, enlisting people in that process, helping them to talk to each other about what they are doing and why, and then getting out of their way and supporting them as they try to get there. This affects the way you design your systems and the way you manage them. You need to have light touch policies and flexible designs so that things can change and develop over time. Much of your work is observing what is happening, seeing what is productive and making that more likely to happen and keep happening. If you get this right people will learn what works, where the high ground is, and how to get there.

Finally – and to stretch the analogy to breaking point – let's be honest – some people are frightened of mice. They see them as unpredictable and hard to control. It is counterintuitive for those more comfortable with large, planned projects to allow things to be speculative and unplanned. They need the assurance of the upfront promise of benefits, they want to know your "route map" and "projected deliverables". You will have to put a lot of effort into assuaging these fears and work to keep people comfortable with your approach. You can describe how this environment works and what its benefits are. There are plenty of examples of businesses that sustain this way of working.

So there is something unassuming and modest about Trojan Mice. You don't have to promise the earth if you are not spending it. Undersell and over deliver. Build small things alongside your more conventional big things. Work at the margins rather than trying to shift the world. Don't throw out your more conventional ways of working but build new ones that fit around them. The mice can run alongside the horses!

Things to remember:

- Deploy small, unobtrusive tools and instigate small changes in practice rather than attempting large scale technological or cultural change.
- Set some Trojan Mice running and obsessively watch what they do. Learn what works and help others to copy it.
- Persuade through results rather than try to convince people in advance and ask for forgiveness rather than permission.
- Keep things "throw away" and inexpensive as long as you can.
- Keep talking about what is working – and what is not – and help people understand your approach.
- You can allow your small projects to grow and flourish alongside more conventional, large ones.

38

DON'T FEED THE TROLLS

Whatever you do in life there will always be someone who has a go at you, finds fault, or does things you wish they didn't. There is something about the online world that makes this more likely. What do you do when the inevitable happens?

This chapter's title refers to trolls. This is the name given online to people who deliberately set out to disrupt things and derail otherwise productive activities. There is something about the online world that makes people less restrained than they might be in normal circumstances. For some this makes them prone to deliberately winding up other people online. Sometimes what looks like trolling is actually just a robust exchange of views and polarized positions. You need difference, and to some extent dissent, to make things interesting but you have to get good at balancing your imbalances. Rough edges and tension make things interesting and a bunch of boring people agreeing with each other about boring stuff sadly sums up many corporate online spaces. But if your dissenters get out of hand their activities can derail other, more productive use of the tools.

One of the most common fears managers have about letting their staff use social tools in the workplace is the prospect of them using the tools to start criticizing the company or finding fault with their management in a relatively public space. This fear is closely followed by the even greater fear of customers having a go at them on the web or – worse still – using the company's own online public spaces to do so. Both fears are usually way out of proportion. The actual number of times either of these scenarios comes to pass is still very, very small. Especially inside the organization people know they are at work. They know they can be identified and know, usually, what is expected of them. In terms of customers finding fault, this probably happens but nine times out of ten it resolves itself fairly quickly. If you have happy customers in the same online space as those criticizing you then your supporters will often manage the situation for you and push back against the critics. If you don't have happy customers who are prepared to do this then maybe you have a bigger problem than dealing with trolls!

In the early days of using social tools in the enterprise, one or two companies made the mistake of allowing anonymous postings on their staff bulletin boards. There were a few widely publicized occasions when this went badly wrong – in one case pretty offensive racist stuff surfaced on an internal forum. Sadly the company in this particular case has yet to fully recover and is still a bit wary of it happening again. The solution is simple: don't allow anonymity on your internal tools (except perhaps for dedicated "whistle blowing" spaces) and make people accountable. They will learn pretty quickly what is OK and what isn't.

Sometimes they are not just being robust in their views or having differences of opinion – they are deliberately setting out to be disruptive. In the context of work this is really not acceptable and you have every right to do something about it. Expose their intentions and most trolls shrink back. They will probably be surprised at someone in their workplace knowing what they are up to! You will always get the occasional nutcase who seems not to care what people think of them, but even this is a benefit. You get to find out who your corporate morons are! Isn't this better than having them sneak up on you and slipping through a job interview? There were several people I made a mental note never to employ as a result of their behaviour on our forum at the BBC.

As with everything else, trolls are more problematic on your public facing sites. Even here though you have every right to do something about them, indeed other users will expect you to. Being seen to judge correctly when and how to intervene can be a very powerful way of establishing your credibility and trustworthiness online. Taking a firm line is OK if you are fair. Trolls disrupt things for everyone and if your online spaces are proving useful to others, being seen to be prepared to police them makes them more attractive to regular users. Explain what you are doing and why. Be consistent. Make sure you are responding to the right problems for the right reasons. If you don't, things will go badly wrong. If you say that you encourage openness and engagement and then subtly or not so subtly jump on anyone who you think is misbehaving, but who other users think is being reasonable, then you can say goodbye to your hopes for frank and open interchange of ideas.

The best way to deal with trolls is to befriend them. Even the worst of them are human. Even if it is some sad loner taking pops at you or your company for no real reason other than having nothing better to do, they have still chosen *your* forum to do it on! They have decided to spend time and energy, however misplaced, in your environment. Tap into this energy. What was it about your space that made them feel it was OK to turn up here? How did they find their way to you? What was it about the way others were behaving that they were attracted to disrupting? Why go to this effort? Yes, sure, you could take the view that they are complete wasters and deserve to be thrown out. Yes, you have the right to do this. But you lose out on so much by doing so. If your critics have shown the energy to engage, and can then be turned around to be supportive of you, then this sends a very strong signal to other dissenters.

Even working out who are dissenters can sometimes be a challenge. I remember talking with clients involved in the nuclear fuels industry in the UK who had a blog which became reasonably popular. They posted news and updates related to nuclear fuel and had a sizeable readership. They allowed comments on their blog and had some active discussions going. Trouble was, some of these discussions got out of hand and not for the reasons you might expect. It wasn't people having a go at nuclear fuel – no, this was actually people supportive of the focus of the blog. People from a particularly strong pro-nuclear fuel lobby in the US regularly took part in the comments and pounced on anyone who dissented from their views. Their enthusiasm for the subject became the problem. In a sense this was a nice problem to have, but it also caused an imbalance in the ecology of the comments and put off other comment-ers. I pointed out that this was straightforward to deal with. This was their blog. It was totally within their rights to manage the blog however they saw fit. Blogs are different from shared spaces like forums where the sense of group ownership is stronger. You own the blog to a higher degree. Yes, explain what you are doing and be fair, but you have every right to be firm too!

There have been a few times over the years on the com-ments on my blog when I have had to deal with trolls and I have always gone out of my way to try to connect at some level. Not all dissenters are trolls. Learn to differentiate. Don't react as if everyone being disruptive is being destruc-tive. Don't get defensive. It is your space that you set up for your reasons and you have the right to make it work a certain way and be used for certain things. Be assertive rather than aggressive. Everyone is watching how you deal with this. It is a wonderful opportunity. Learn to love your trolls and turn them into your friends!

Things to remember:

- Trolls are those who set out to disrupt otherwise productive activities online.
- Online conversations tend to be more robust than face to face and sometimes it is difficult to tell the difference between lively exchanges, which you want, and disruptive behaviour, which you don't.
- Usually there are enough constraints within organizations so that internal conversations don't get out of hand.
- If they do, you get to find out who your troublemakers are!
- In your public facing spaces, if you have cultivated a healthy community spirit, your supporters will help you deal with troublemakers.
- It is important that you are seen to deal with trolls firmly as it is in the interests of your other users.
- Often it is possible to get behind why people are causing trouble, tap into their energy, and get them on your side.

39

WHEN THE SHIT HITS
THE FAN

Despite your best efforts, your business will at some time be criticized on the Internet. Better to learn how to deal with it before it happens rather than after.

A lot of organizations are very wary of social media because they are afraid of communication with their staff or customers "getting out of control". They fear the rogue member of staff ranting on their internal forums or worse still being indiscreet on the web. They dread customers criticizing them and damaging their brand. Highly publicized examples of both of these apparent risks don't help. The thing to understand is that they never really had control in the first place. The world of channels and managed communications gave the impression of control, but people could always have conversations around the water cooler or in the pub – it was just that you weren't aware of it. What these new tools give you on the other hand is much more important – they give you a vastly improved ability to influence.

Talking to someone in the financial sector recently, he was expressing frustration at the negative gossip on blogs about his organization, and the willingness of the press to pick up on or even encourage this. Setting aside the changing role of the press for the moment, I suggested that the best defence was to get his version of the truth out there on blogs and build a network of people who believed what he said and trusted his credibility. If enough people trust and believe him then they will push back against, or ignore, those who are polluting the system with negativity or noise. The system will want to self-correct if you help it to. Having the confidence to talk openly about your position preemptively is the best form of defence. Make your message more compelling, trustworthy, and effective and people will support you. Fill the web with sanitized corporate platitudes and they won't.

But what if the worst does happen? What matters most is how you respond to the thing that has gone wrong. If you are seen to deal with the aftermath of a PR disaster fairly and honestly, for example, it can turn into a real opportunity. Shit happens and no one expects otherwise. It is a classic in customer relations that recovery is a valuable way of enhancing brand and credibility.

As another example, when I was working with NATO they expressed frustration at the media focusing on telling sensational stories when they got things wrong rather than showing any interest at all in the ongoing good work that they do. In cases like this, you should grab the moral high ground by telling your own good news stories in compelling ways and building a network of people positively disposed to what you do. Be as open and as honest as you can. People's expectations are so low that if you explain why you can't talk about certain topics they will understand and accept your position if they trust you. If military bloggers blog well and build trust then other bloggers will pick up and amplify their perspective, making it more likely that mainstream media will eventually pick up on their more positive stories.

Being willing to learn from your mistakes is a strength. If your customers are expressing dissatisfaction on the web don't run away from them, take part in the conversation. Yes there are times when saying nothing is the best policy, and a lot of negativity blows over if you don't fan the flames, but if there is a genuine concern, others on the web will be able to see this and make their own decisions. You are far better to engage with the situation than do nothing and hope it will go away. Make your disaster recovery better than everyone else's. Earn a reputation for taking criticism on the chin and dealing with your problems – people will love you for it. If you have a product or service that people love then you have little to fear. If you don't then the problem is not the Internet or social media but your business or product itself. That is what you have to deal with, and in many ways being forced to do so by some sort of issue is not in the long term a bad thing.

It might seem easier to get an external agency to manage your disasters for you but this can be problematic. Yes there is a skill to managing relationships with the public but you are also introducing a third party. One of the themes of this book has been to find your own, authentic, voice. It's much better to build up your ability to look after yourself when things go wrong rather than to rely on others. A lot of people are jumping on the social media bandwagon these days and offering advice without necessarily having fully understood the way the web works. You are likely to be able to learn at least as fast as they are. Many of them still try to manage situations through conventional channels and don't know how to influence through online networks. Also having a horde of PR folks pretending to be you and rushing to your defence is going to be found out and will almost certainly blow back in your face.

Start building your networks and relationships now. Don't wait until things go wrong. If you only ever use Twitter when things have already gone pear shaped, and don't show a willingness to hang around for the longer term relationships, then you would be better not to use it. On the other hand if you have been able to establish yourselves online, and are trusted, then when things go wrong people will be willing to listen to you and give you the benefit of the doubt.

Learning can sometimes be hard and it can hurt. Doing this in public is not trivial and can hurt at an individual level. In fact the fear of making mistakes in public or saying the wrong thing is one of the reasons that people are wary of using social tools. But often the greatest learning comes out of the things that hurt the most. If we are able to be interested in what is happening to us, even when that is hard and unpleasant, then the worst situation can become a learning opportunity. If we can then find the courage to blog about what went wrong and how we feel about this then people will love us for it. Those facing the same challenges will learn along with you and those on the brink will admire your bravery and honesty. You really can turn the worst that can happen into the best that can happen and show others that it is not so much what happens that matters, as what you do about it.

Things to remember:

- If it was ever possible to control messages it certainly isn't now, but on the other hand you have greater opportunity to influence than ever before.
- Take part online, get people on your side, and influence them before things go wrong – not after.
- If you tell your story well and build trust then people will support you when things go wrong.
- Beware of getting other people to talk for you – it rarely works.
- Be as open and honest as you can, and if you deal well with things when they go wrong this will be seen as a real strength.

40

CRISIS MANAGEMENT

Social media tools are ideal for communicating during unpredictable situations. Their universality and flexibility have been seen to be effective in numerous global disasters. You can learn to use them for crisis management too.

Various worldwide disasters, from the tsunami in the Indian Ocean to the flooding in Louisiana, showed a whole new way to respond to crises. The ability to set up blogs and wikis using free web tools had never been put to this use before and we marvelled at the role they played in helping people find information and support while the official systems struggled to get going and have relevance. This is because when things are out of control you can't always guarantee that the right person with the right role and the right permissions gets to the right system at the right time. Attempts to take an official position hamper the ability to react. In contrast, individuals on the web, able to flock around tools like wikis, can easily contribute what they know and collectively work out what is happening and what to do about it.

It has always struck me as odd that we try to plan for the unpredictable which, by its very nature, is hard to predict. We build systems based on rigid procedures and roles and imagine that the next thing to go wrong is going to be pretty much like the last. Disaster recovery systems assign roles and responsibilities before the event and our technology then creates rigid information flows. These measures are meant to make our responses to disasters "efficient" – more often than not they make them ridiculous. In contrast, being able to give context to events as they happen is effective. Why is this happening? What is the background? What did we do last time? Having this available to you as you face a crisis will be invaluable. If it is available at people's fingertips as they need it, it is all the more powerful. Better still, more relevant information faster is just what you need when the shit hits the fan and this is just what social tools are able to deliver.

No one is saying that you throw away your official systems, but changing the way they work may help to get the best of both worlds. Allow those dealing with the emergency to use social tools alongside their official system. Help them to cross boundaries into the unofficial online world if they need to pick up on weak signals from those close to what is happening. You will eventually need to have an official and effective response, but you will be doing it in the context of better and faster information gained in those important early days. You will also be able to do it with more resource at your disposal as those who are close to the situation and able to help will be in a position to identify themselves to you. Planning for this is different from conventional disaster recovery planning. It will require thought and experience to get it right. But it can happily work alongside more conventional ways of dealing with disasters and enhance the more structured approaches we are familiar with.

Indeed if you use social tools to formulate your processes and procedures in the first place, you are less likely to have disasters and better able to handle them when they happen. The lead roles will change. Being in charge will change. Yes you will need some sort of structure to determine authority, but those with the authority will make their decisions based on a far richer range of inputs than currently. They will also use social tools to discuss what they are doing and why so that the ability to reality check and get feedback is constant and ongoing. Tweeting about what you are doing to recover a situation gives others the opportunity to reality check your decisions and add their own information and perspectives to your solution.

You should be open enough to accept help and input from wherever it is offered. You must take advantage of serendipity and not stand on ceremony as to whether or not it is someone's job to be getting involved. A flatter structure and more egalitarian culture is most likely to accommodate a range of perspectives on your solution, whereas a small group of isolated experts is going to struggle to get everything right all the time. Conducting more of your response online also allows you to check back on what you did and why. Being able to look back over a fast moving Twitter thread in a disaster situation can give valuable context to where you are now. The ability to track back over your actions and make adjustments is live. Some people may lead in the early days when they have energy and insight, to be replaced by others when they start to flag. Allow people to use the system to manage the running of the system. If you have enough people who trust each other and know what is going on then they can become self-managing and thereby increase the speed of their decisions.

The same principles apply to less extreme disasters such as PR nightmares or systems failure in businesses. Having networks of people who can pick up on something as it is going wrong, quickly work out together what the real situation is, and start working together on what do about it will become an essential part of disaster recovery planning. Even as individuals, more and more of us use tools like Twitter to keep up to date with risky and fast changing situations. We work as networks to establish what is happening and what to do about it. Whether dealing with large scale disasters, bad corporate PR, or personal situations involving risk, having access to fast information you can trust and on which you can base your moment to moment decisions is a key part of dealing with the unpredictable aspects of life. But start to build those networks and trust before your disaster happens – not afterwards.

Things to remember: `

■ The flexibility of social tools has played a part in helping people deal with a number of major natural disasters.

■ Don't expect rigid systems to be good at dealing with unpredictable situations.

■ Use social tools to enhance your more substantive crisis recovery systems.

■ Be flexible in who you call on for help and engage the wider web wherever possible.

■ Build your networks and capability before things go wrong, not after.

41

THE BEST WAY TO BE SAFE IS TO BE OPEN

Security is, in many organizations, the last bastion of IT power and influence, but what are we so afraid of? Are our worries about security limiting our ability to work? Might using social tools be the safest thing we could do?

Fears about security are amongst the reasons most frequently given for not allowing the use of social media in organizations. The perceived risk is presumably that allowing people to use these tools while at work makes it easier for them to be indiscreet and share inappropriate information. There are a couple of problems with this – which people are we talking about and what is our current definition of "at work"?

Firstly who is it that leaks important information from organizations? Is it the lowly member of staff "wasting time" on Twitter – or is it the senior executive poached by a competitor specifically for his ability and willingness to share with them what he knows about your organization? In truth it is anyone who has become disaffected enough with your organization to wish to do you damage.

The second problem is with "at work". Increasingly people are "working" at all times of the day or night – any time they can get a connection to the Internet. This can be at work, at home on their work computer, at home on their own computer, or even in a local cafe on their smart phone. The clear lines between what is at work and what is not have long gone. Likewise the firewall. Organizations still have firewalls, the technology that keeps the intranet separated from the Internet, but that line is getting more and more blurred. As companies outsource more of their activities, the bits that appear to be part of the organization but are actually outside the firewall increasingly outnumber the bits that are inside.

So if the lines are getting blurred how do you police them? Most take a technological approach and place all sorts of restrictions on what services or web sites can be accessed from work. The trouble with this is that you end up with the IT department making what can appear to be random decisions that then inhibit the ability to get work done. People are forever finding work-arounds for these sorts of restrictions and their inventive efforts ironically make the systems more at risk rather than less. The most effective way to manage security is through education. Explain to people what is secure and what is risky. Help them to make better judgements about their actions and give them good reasons to do the right thing.

Paradoxically, for those opposed to social tools in the workplace, using a blog to update people and explain the nuances of security is one of the best ways of improving your ability to stay safe. Before starting to blog the BBC IT security team were frankly seen by many of us as the guys who liked to say no to anything remotely useful or interesting. Once they started blogging we became much more aware of the challenges they were facing and more sympathetic to the need to curtail some of what we wanted to do. Their interesting and well written blog became very popular and their credibility, and ability to have influence, improved significantly. In fact many of us became interested enough in what they were doing to work with them to discover ways to help them meet their challenges.

Make security something that people take ownership of. Allow people to discuss security. As an example, when the Freedom of Information Act became law, there were a lot of us concerned as to what impact it would have on our internal forum at the BBC. Would it mean we had to avoid certain topics? Would it mean we would have to close the forum down? Frankly we didn't know the answers and were milling around in the dark. Except that we weren't milling around in the dark – we were doing it on a forum visible to all staff. As a result the expert deployed by the BBC to manage the legislation became aware of our online conversations and began to take part. He did so very well and became a real part of our ongoing attempts to understand the legislation, responding to our questions and explaining some of the reasons behind the rules. The result was that, through these visible conversations, thousands of BBC staff had a really good idea about this particular set of rules and how to stick to them. In contrast, the conventional way to attempt this would be to issue memos to managers who may or may not pass them on to their staff, and people – if they did read them – would have to pretty much work them out for themselves.

A counterintuitive angle on security is that being open is your best defence. Share as much as you can as soon as you can and you will find that all sorts of problems begin to go away. We tend to have very blanket approaches to deciding what can be shared and our position starts from nothing and works from there. Where possible, sharing as much as you can, when you are able to do so, means that people are more likely to respect you when you say you can't share some information. If you are seen to have trusted both your staff and the outside world, then they are much less likely to abuse that trust. Building trust and managing expectations are much more cost effective ways of managing security than IT solutions.

Even if you do leak – it is rarely the end of the world. How you deal with your leak matters more than the fact that the leak happened, and in some cases being seen to be big enough to be open earns you the best PR you could hope for. The main point to make is that we have to take a collective organizational responsibility for security and be big enough to learn from our mistakes. Rather than punishing people for breaking rules they would have been hard pushed to be aware of, enlist their help and support in making your organization secure.

Things to remember:

- We often take an overly simplistic, all or nothing approach to security which gets translated into unworkably confining technical solutions.
- Security is at least as much a cultural issue as a technical one.
- Help people to take ownership of security.
- Use social tools to talk about security and engage your staff on the subject.
- If you default to open rather than closed, share as much information as you can when you can, and build the trust of your staff and customers – then they will be more likely to accept any limits you place on what can or can't be talked about.

42

RADICAL TRANSPARENCY

Thanks to technology, transparency – both inside organizations and between organizations and those they serve – has become a big issue. How do you cope with your business communications if everything you say might one day be made public knowledge?

If the best way to be safe is to be open – how far can you push this? It is a slightly facile response, but when asked years ago where my office shredder was, I responded that I had a much more cost effective solution – I didn't say anything I regretted that much. In fact online I recommend that people assume that if you have written something on a computer then someone else will at some time be able to see it. If you don't want someone to see what you have written, don't write it on a computer. Does this mean you can't write about anything? No, but it does mean you have to think harder about what you are writing, where, and why. Am I allowed to say what I am writing? Am I happy with what I am writing? Am I prepared to stand by it in the future? What do I expect people to do with what I have written and who do I expect to read it? This accountability and thoughtfulness is not a bad thing.

Transparency inside organizations isn't easy. In fact one of the biggest risks is people sharing things inadvertently. Corporate document systems attempt to manage what is visible to whom, but managing this is a challenge. In addition people are naïve about search and assume that everyone wants to be able to search everything. Not so. What I am happy with you seeing now I might not be in six months because one of us has changed roles, the project may have moved into a different phase, your whole division may have been outsourced. How do I keep track of this? Do I keep track of it or do I trust IT and some role based system?

And what if people steal what you know? In the BBC, programme ideas are gold dust – they can launch your career if you get a good idea and get to make the programme. Consequently people have tended to keep such things very close to their chests over the years. One day on our forum, which was visible to all 25,000 or so staff, someone posted a programme idea. You could almost hear the collective intake of breath at such a rash act. As soon as the posting appeared, another member of staff responded by asking if the poster wasn't worried about someone stealing their idea. However another then chipped in pointing out that no one could steal the idea because the original poster had just claimed it as his in front of 25,000 people!

The benefits, both to the individual and the organization, of increased openness mean that, on balance, I believe it is better to assume open as your default rather than closed. Assume that anyone can read anything you write except in exceptional circumstances when you then treat things very differently. Instead of having over managed and over complicated IT solutions to prevent people seeing what you write, make more of what you write more accessible in the first place. There will be those who will say that I am being naïve, and clearly this approach is not applicable in all business circumstances, but it is practical in more cases than most people believe. In fact radical transparency may be your best form of defence. When everything is a copy and paste away from another part of the intranet – or even the Internet – everything can ultimately be discovered anyway. Why not be open and up front in the first place? The consequences of being more open with our communications are significant, but to close things down removes our ability to do business.

Being open isn't easy. How do we feel about being totally open as individuals? Many people are very reticent about blogging because they think they have to blog about everything they do. Let's get one thing straight – just because you have a blog doesn't mean you develop verbal diarrhoea. You don't have to write about everything all of the time. For instance I am careful about how much I write about family or clients as they need to be able to trust me to be discreet. If I am not, our relationships would quickly break down.

However you can write about more than you might think. A lot of what we might usefully share is not contentious. Even for more sensitive things you can blog about the interesting and salient points of an incident or meeting without giving away all of the details. You can extract the essence and the learning without giving anything confidential away. Some people are very good at being interesting and open about what they do without compromising their situations. East London ambulance driver Tom Reynolds is a prime example of this. In his blog *Random Acts of Reality*, Tom extracted the interesting essence of the routine of his job as an East London paramedic but managed to write about it in such a way that his bosses trusted him and saw the benefits rather than the risks in his openness. Tom was so good at this that his blog was eventually turned into a book and subsequently formed the basis of a drama on Channel 4!

The opportunities for networking and building relationships increase with openness. How do people know they can help you if you don't let them know what you are struggling with? There is a reticence about openness in society generally and even more so in business. We have all felt discomfort at people being too open at the wrong time to the wrong people, and in fact a lot of the initial reaction to blogs was "who cares what you think and what happened to you today?" An elderly relative once said to me "Oh yes blogging, isn't that a lot of people just expressing their opinions?" Well, yes it is, and what is so wrong with that? We talk about knowledge sharing but then get squeamish about openness – we can't have one without the other.

One of the advantages of being more transparent is increased accountability. If it is clear what you have done, and why, people are more likely to trust you. The more open you have been, the less risk there is of something difficult being exposed. What are people so worried about anyway? What dreadful things is your company doing? There is an uncomfortable bottom line about openness and its impact on business – as Dave Winer, the inventor of RSS, once said: "If you don't want me to slag off your product on the Internet, don't have a shit product." Being seen as being confident enough as a business, or an individual, to be open about what you are doing and why can be a great strength and a great way to build brand. Increasingly the opposite is going to look dodgy and work against you. For me, one of the most exciting prospects of transparency inside organizations is that we can spread the responsibility. If enough people know what is going on and enough small quiet voices get to go "Are we sure we should be doing this?" then maybe we would avoid some of the worst corporate excesses and dodgy decisions.

Things to remember:

- Assume that anything that you have written on a computer may at some point be seen by someone else.
- Being as open as possible is not only easier and cheaper – it is also ironically safer.
- Being open in a business context is unfamiliar and challenging, but maintaining a closed world is difficult and counterproductive.
- Just because you have a blog doesn't mean you have to tell everyone everything.
- Being open allows us to share more and makes it easier for people to help us.
- Openness brings with it accountability and this makes organizations and individuals stronger rather than weaker.

43

THE REVOLUTION IS WITHIN

The biggest change that we will see in business is not in the systems we use, the strategies we adopt, or even the organizational structures we invent. The biggest difference is going to be inside ourselves. In our sense of self, what that means in terms of work, and how we use the workplace as the best opportunity we have to discover what we are capable of as individuals.

When you have a conventional Taylorist view of the workplace you see your staff as relatively undifferentiated bits of meatware that you strap to your machines to get them to work. In the post industrial world we have "employee engagement" and other mealy mouthed attempts to re-invent the language of the workplace to be more acceptable to people who have realized that there is more to life than being a wage slave. But this linguistic tinkering at the edges is being perpetrated by people who really haven't moved on from the idea that the organization is a thing, has an existence outside of the people who work in it, and can consume "human resources" albeit in a more socially acceptable way.

In reality organizations have only ever been loosely held networks of individuals who turn up at the same place at the same time. They do so for a complex mix of reasons, most of which are personal – and have little to do with money. It is these aspects of being at work that begin to become more apparent when you start to use social media. The assumptions about work weaken. We see more variation and complexity. The subtlety of motivation becomes more apparent and simplistic approaches to management begin to struggle.

Once people start writing their ideas down and making them visible to others they get into really interesting feedback loops. What one writer thinks is obvious may be not so obvious to other people who read their blog posts. The assumptions held by senior management may not be held by those beneath them. When you are faced with the fact that not everyone sees the world the way you do, how does this make you feel? Are you happy to have a different perspective? Do you think you might change your position slightly? We don't really have these sorts of thoughtful exchanges normally in the workplace. It is very much nose to the grindstone and thinking is seen as a waste of time.

The prevailing wisdom in the workplace is "don't stand around navel gazing – do something". Maybe we want to move towards "don't just do something – stand there"? Maybe being thoughtful might just be productive?

There is something fundamental about writing more thoughtfully online – journaling – that reveals us to ourselves. By writing about the workplace you become more thoughtful about your place in it and what it does for you. What relationships exist and what do they do to help or hinder your ability to get things done? What price do you pay psychologically for doing what you do? What growth does your career afford you? What do you learn about yourself and your colleagues from being at work? What dark and difficult parts of yourself does work force you to address? I have often thought that targeted strategic therapy to cure some of the most dysfunctional behaviour in the workplace would have more of a beneficial effect than the management initiatives we are so often subjected to. Blogging might be the most cost effective way to achieve the same end. Thoughtful, self aware managers might be just what your organization needs to move forward.

As an individual resolving and dealing with your challenges in a more thoughtful way you will be more energized and committed to your work – or if you can't be, you will have the confidence to move. You will start to get better at whatever it is you do as you become more thoughtful and share more of your knowledge with others. You will see those around you doing the same thing and be encouraged to continue on this new and exciting path. If you are a manager you will be able to see what your staff are thinking and be better placed to understand your own role in that. How do people react to you? Are you able to motivate people to do their best? How do you deal with it when they don't? Being self-aware and thoughtful about our impact on the world is one of our most important opportunities for growth. The workplace is such a large part of our lives that to pass through it without seriously thinking about what it means seems such a waste.

By changing within we can change what is outside. In fact this is the only way we can change what is outside – despite decades of management theory to the contrary. Blogging can help people to understand themselves and their work better and by doing so help them to change at a profound and fundamental level. Once more people become more self-aware you will be amazed at what starts to happen. Sure there will be an initial period of awkwardness, but over time tensions will reduce, energy will increase, and disputes will be resolved more quickly. In effect we will start to grow up and take responsibility for ourselves at work. The victim mentality of so many who are "employed" doesn't help them or the business. Networks of engaged, thoughtful, self-aware, and tolerant staff have got to be the way to become more efficient and, more importantly, more effective. People taking responsibility for themselves and their part in the enterprise for the first time.

Things to remember:

- Organizations are not machines – they are networks of people.
- As an individual, the process of writing about your work changes your work.
- Having a thoughtful culture makes your organization more effective.
- Groups of grown-ups being more thoughtful about their work become more able and willing to resolve issues and learn from each other.

44

IT'S *YOUR* PARTY . . .

If you are going to do anything online it has to be yours. It is coming directly from you. Not from your company, not from your role, from you. Wear your heart on your sleeve, join the party, and enjoy yourself.

Whether it is your blog, or forum post at work, or Facebook page, or tweet at home, this is your thing. You have to own it. It is yours. It is you. Many people get jumpy about this. It may be the first time they have put themselves down in writing. Committed, made public. Exposed. But then this is also why we do it. It makes you think harder. If you are going to say what you think in public you have to become happy about what you are thinking. If you are not happy about what you are saying, don't say it and do something about it until you are happy. This is the bottom line message of this book.

In many ways blogging is a bit like being a student. For many of us, the main benefit of being a student was that you got to play at being different types of people. Play at being a grown-up in different ways before you have to do it for real. We all play at being different people. We are different when we are at work from when we are at home. We are different when we are angry from when we are happy. There is no real us. We are making it up as we go along. With a blog you are doing some of that 'making it up' in public. This is not easy but it is a good thing. You have to think harder about what you think and why. There is something about committing to your ideas in public that makes you grow up.

Many years ago I got to meet Vint Cerf, one of the "fathers of the Internet". I was with him when he was asked by a journalist "Do you think, looking back, that the Internet has been a good or a bad thing?" To this he replied "It is just a thing. Whether it is good or bad depends on what you are doing with it. If you don't like what you are doing with it then that is a reflection of what you are as an individual, an organization or a society. That is what you have to do something about."

You need to stand up for yourself and to be prepared to stand by your ideas when they are examined, picked over, and possibly ridiculed. Even having people love your ideas can be challenging. If you have written about a tentative idea or something speculative and people pick it up, run with it, and turn it into a big thing it can be scary. Your idea takes on a life of its own. One of the points of using social tools at work is that you speed up the evolutionary process, and when it is your own evolution that is being speeded up it can be scary. It has consequences.

You need to be prepared to live with the consequences of what you say. It is about saying, "It's my party and I'll cry if I want to." And that is the other big thing – emotion. If you write without emotion you might as well write a memo. Blogs have attitude and voice. Moving the emotional needle on a forum gets a reaction. You have to invest yourself in this writing for it to have impact and an effect.

This is one of the most exposing aspects of what I've been talking about in this book. Not only am I saying that you have to have opinions and express them but also that you are going to have to do so with passion. This is the antithesis of the cold, rational, third person business memo. This is up to your elbows, working it out, messily moving things on.

You learn to be assertive in a really healthy way. You learn to become comfortable with what you think and why. You will also become happier with how you relate to others. Remember those teenage parties when you were terrified that people wouldn't like you? The need to fit in and be cool? That mix of being confident enough to throw a party but then not confident enough to deal with how well, or badly, it goes. Having a blog is about that feeling.

If you are running a "community" you have this challenge too. What if things go wrong at your party? Dissent in an online forum that you are responsible for is like having a party when your parents are out and watching your friends trash their house. You want people to have a good time at the party. You want them to get on with you. You want them to get on with each other. In fact the role of running online communities is very like the traditional role of society host. You need to get good at inviting the right people and encouraging them to mix. You take responsibility for making sure that everyone has a good time and you do something about it if they don't. You become known for running good parties and people turn up when you host them. In fact your parties are the places to be seen and you are known as someone who gets the best out of people and helps them to have a good time while doing so.

So this is your party – is it going to be good one? Are you going to put in the effort and energy to make it a success? Lurkers make up the vast majority of the online population, and there is nothing wrong with being the online equivalent of a wall flower, but good party hosts make sure that as many people get involved as possible and leave the party feeling that it was worth their while coming. So be social in your use of online tools. Wear your heart on your sleeve and attract interesting, energetic people to your online gatherings. Be brave enough to open up and be yourself, to connect with other people and share your ideas and your passions. And don't forget to help other people to do the same.

Things to remember:

- It is important to own your online presence. Make the most of the opportunity and learn to say what you think.
- It is scary being yourself online and opening up to a wider audience than ever before.
- Be playful about discovering the "real you" online.
- Be willing to engage with others in this process of discovery.
- Don't be afraid to introduce some passion into what you say. Commit and be energetic.
- Parties raise energy and help people to connect – so do social tools.
- Be good at including others in whatever you do online. Make it social. Make your parties better than everyone else's!

45

A FINAL WORD

It seems appropriate to end this book with a blog post. A blog post that I wrote as I left the BBC after working there for twenty-one years. A blog post in which I talk about love – the force that makes everything hang together.

A Word or Two on Love

THURSDAY, MARCH 9, 2006 AT 4:12PM

Some time back David Weinberger wrote that the motivating force behind the internet was love. It was the basic human desire to connect that made it all hang together. At the time I admired his idealism and indeed bravery at being so open about something we have all been trained to dismiss as at best personal and at worst a sign of weakness.

In contrast I have just finished reading Joel Balkan's *The Corporation* in which he exposes the fact that corporations are legally bound to do just one thing – maximise shareholder value and that in fact to be motivated by higher ideals, or indeed love, could be considered detrimental to that overriding purpose if it impacts the bottom line in anything but a positive way.

Where did all this come from, where did the idea that the most powerfully motivating force in the world had nothing to do with business? We spend most of our adult lives in the workplace and at work we bring about the most important and long lasting changes to our society and our planet – and yet we are not encouraged to talk in terms of love. OK we just about get away with "loving our job" or "loving success" but start talking about loving colleagues or loving customers and you'll have people running for the door. And yet isn't this what makes great people and great places tick? A deep sense of connection with each other, a depth of purpose beyond the everyday that sees customers as more than merely stepping stones on the way to returning that value to the shareholders?

A couple of weeks ago we had a closing down party for DigiLab, my small but perfectly formed department at the BBC, and the next morning I started to write a post about love at work and what a powerful motivating force it can be. But I stopped myself. I let myself be influenced by those grown up voices in my head telling me not to be so silly – certainly not in public! But the warmth and affection we felt for each other, for our physical space in Television Centre and yes, sorry guys, for the punters who we dealt with on a daily basis over the years had more to do with love than anything else I can think of and certainly little to do with those extrinsic motivators – money, corporate goals and efficiency that we we were meant to have taken so seriously.

Love is also the powerful force you unleash when you start to introduce social computing inside organisations. Hugh Macleod wrote a while back about the disruptive effects you should expect but the disruption results from stronger stuff. The stuff David was talking of. The desire to connect at a very deep human level. To see colleagues as intrinsically linked and capable of pulling together in ways that those who promulgated scarcity and competition as organisational drivers will never begin to understand.

Over the last four years of watching the BBC's internal forums grow to their current population of half the organisation I have seen so many examples of love and connection – some of which made the hairs on the back of my neck stand on end. I mean real examples of people selflessly helping each other, genuine affection and concern shown between people who more often than not never physically met, and as one of the participants once said a greater sense of 'one BBC' than any of the corporate initiatives that came and went over the years.

Maybe love does have a place in business after all. Maybe more and more of us will start to have the courage to begin to talk about what really matters to us about work and our relationships with each other and to push back the sterile language of business that we have been trained to accept. Maybe we will realise that accepting love into the workplace reminds us of the original purpose of work – not to maximise shareholder value but to come together to do good things, to help each other and hopefully to make the world a better place.

Maybe. . . .

Oh and by the way if the above is too new age and namby pamby for you I reckon social computing is capable of taking 25% out of the running costs of most businesses – so there!

Thank you for sticking with me to the end. I hope you have learned something on the way and will feel encouraged to get involved. Have fun with whatever you do online and use it to help us build a better world. You can always find me at euansemple.com if you ever want to get in touch.

A NOTE
ABOUT TECHNOLOGY

Ithought it might be useful to have a list of the tools that we have talked about in the book. This isn't meant to be an exhaustive list, and will almost certainly be out of date within the life of the book, but it should at the very least let you know what I meant throughout the book when I have referred to "these tools".

Forums

Sometimes called a bulletin board or newsgroup, a forum is a place where people can post questions or statements and get answers or discussion from any of the other users in the system. Originally based on mailing lists and then Usenet, forums have been developed a lot recently and tools like Yahoo Groups and Google Groups have added in diary, file sharing, user profiles etc. to make them much richer collaborative environments. Forum functionality is also now built into sites like LinkedIn, Google Plus, and Facebook. Our forum was the first tool we put in at the BBC which eventually grew to around 25,000 users and despite being less glamorous than some of the more modern tools is still a great engine on which to build your ecology of tools.

Weblogs

Weblogs are simply online journals but there are a number of things that make them significant. Firstly they are really the first time that it has been trivially easy to publish into a web environment. Until now you have had to be geeky enough to write code or pay for dedicated applications. With a weblog (blog) you use your web browser to access free, or cheap, blogging tools, write your content, press "save" and your content is published onto the web.

The second significant thing about weblogs was the per-malink. With normal web sites, pointing at content was a risky business as re-designs or changes of content could break those links. With a blog, each post has a unique and persistent url that makes that content linkable to for the life of the blog. This simple fact enables rich lines of thought to be built up between different blogs or within the same blog. For all their simplicity blogs are, in many ways, still the most powerful social media tool.

Social networking tools

Within the last few years there has been a spate of tools building on the idea of yellow pages where users upload information about themselves and their interests and can then form groups and associations with other users. The popularity of Google Plus, Facebook, and LinkedIn particularly has been phenomenal, but at their most basic they add colour and depth to someone's online presence and make it easy to surface informal associations and connections. We had a precursor to these web services inside the BBC and there are now a number of commercial options if you want to build this capability inside the firewall. There are also an increasing number of "Enterprise 2.0" solutions which have this functionality at their core but for reasons given elsewhere in this book I would be wary of one size fits all solutions.

Wikis

Wikis are basically collaboratively written online documents. They make it easy for groups to write, edit, link, or delete pages in a way that enables collaborative working as never before. The word isn't an acronym as many people assume but comes from the Hawaiian phrase "wiki wiki" which means quickly. A number of features are common to most wiki tools. The history of each page's changes is tracked and can be seen by all users. Differences between versions are represented graphically and it is easy to revert to previous versions of each page.

The power of wiki technology is most clearly seen in Wikipedia where users have created and sustained millions of pages (that is just in English – Wikipedia also has versions in more than a hundred languages) to create an encyclopaedia to rival the *Encyclopaedia Britannica* in depth and accuracy. We used wikis in the BBC to produce all sorts of official and semi-official documentation from policies to guidelines and even including some scripts.

Twitter

Twitter is a microblogging service that can be accessed via text, web, or SMS. It allows networks of users to stay connected and update each other on their activities wherever they are. Most people's initial reaction to Twitter is of unleashed inanity, but once you have invested time in building interesting and useful networks it is a real aid to productivity and knowledge sharing. There are now Twitter clones, such as Yammer, suitable for use within the corporate environment.

RSS

RSS stands for "Really Simple Syndication" and is a method for weblogs, wikis, or forums to publish their content in a way that readers can then subscribe to it. This allows readers to select sites they value, subscribe to their content, and be alerted in applications called aggregators when that content has changed. They can then read the various content from these diverse sources in their aggregator, removing the need to visit lots of sources and try to keep track of what has changed since the last time they were visited.

RSS is fundamental to building a knowledge sharing environment using these tools and brings about possibly the biggest shift in behaviour. Web content becomes streams and patterns of new and relevant stories rather than static, unrelated content. Users who get expert at finding "the good stuff" can share their RSS subscriptions with others and help them piggy back on their experience and valuable sources of news and information.

READING LIST

The following is a list of books that I have enjoyed reading and that have helped form the opinions in this book. Some relate directly to its content and others indirectly but I love book lists that give me a possibility of further exploration so I hope you find something here to pique your interest.

Abrahamson, Eric, and David H. Freedman. *A Perfect Mess: The Hidden Benefits of Disorder*. Phoenix, 2007.

Ahonen, Tomi T., and Alan Moore. *Communities Dominate Brands: Business and Marketing Challenges for the 21st Century*. Futuretext, 2005.

Allen, David. *Getting Things Done: The Art of Stress-Free Productivity*. Penguin Books, 2003.

Babauta, Leo. *Power of Less, The: The Fine Art of Limiting Yourself to the Essential*. Hyperion, 2009.

Benkler, Y. *The Wealth of Networks: How Social Production Transforms Markets and Freedom*. Yale University Press, 2007.

Berners-Lee, Tim, and Mark Fischetti. *Weaving the Web: The Original Design and Ultimate Destiny of the World Wide Web by Its Inventor*. Harper San Francisco, 1999.

Buchanan, Mark. *Small World: Uncovering Nature's Hidden Networks*. Phoenix, 2003.

Carpenter, Sam. *Work the System: The Simple Mechanics of Making More and Working Less*. Greenleaf Book Group LLC, 2009.

Castells, Manuel. *Communication Power*. OUP Oxford, 2009.

Chandler, Steve. *100 Ways To Motivate Yourself: Change Your Life Forever*. Career Press, 2004.

Downes, Larry. *The Laws of Disruption Chaos: Harnessing the New Forces that Govern Life and Business in the Digital Age.* Basic Books, 2009.

Gawande, Atul. *The Checklist Manifesto: How To Get Things Right.* Profile Books, 2010.

Gladwell, Malcolm. *The Tipping Point: How Little Things Can Make a Big Difference.* Abacus, 2002.

Godin, Seth. *Permission Marketing: Turning Strangers into Friends and Friends into Customers.* Pocket Books, 2007.

Hafner, Katie, and Matthew Lyon. *Where Wizards Stay Up Late: The Origins of the Internet.* Simon & Schuster, 1998.

Hodgkinson, Tom. *The Freedom Manifesto: How to Free Yourself from Anxiety, Fear, Mortgages, Money, Guilt, Debt, Government, Boredom, Supermarkets, Bills, Mela.* Harper Perennial, 2007.

Jarvis, Jeff. *What Would Google Do?.* Collins, 2009.

Jarvis, Jeff. *Public Parts: How Sharing in the Digital Age Improves the Way We Work and Live.* Simon & Schuster, 2011.

Johnson, Steven. *Emergence: The Connected Lives of Ants, Brains, Cities and Software.* Penguin, 2002.

Johnson, Steven. *Everything Bad Is Good for You: How Popular Culture Is Making Us Smarter.* Allen Lane, 2005.

Kelly, Kevin. *Out of Control: The New Biology of Machines, Social Systems, and the Economic World.* Perseus Books, 1995.

Kelly, Kevin. *What Technology Wants.* Viking Books, 2010.

Lessig, Lawrence. *Code: And Other Laws of Cyberspace.* Basic Books, 1999.

Levine, Rick, et al. *The Cluetrain Manifesto.* Basic Books, 2009.

Levy, David M. *Scrolling Forward: Making Sense of Documents in the Digital Age.* Arcade Publishing, 2003.

Locke, Christopher. *Gonzo Marketing.* Perseus Books, 2001.

Maxwell, John C. *Failing Forward: Turning Mistakes into Stepping Stones for Success.* Nelson Business an imprint of Thomas Nelson Publishers, 2007.

McLuhan, Marshall. *Understanding Media.* Routledge, 2001.

Peters, Thomas J. *Thriving on Chaos: Handbook for a Management Revolution.* Pan Books, 1989.

Postrel, Virginia. *The Future and Its Enemies: The Growing Conflict over Creativity, Enterprise and Progress.* Pocket Books, 1999.

Rheingold, Howard. *Smart Mobs: The Next Social Revolution.* Perseus Books, U.S., 2003.

Shirky, Clay. *Here Comes Everybody.* Allen Lane, 2008.

Stacey, Ralph. *Complex Responsive Processes in Organizations: Learning and Knowledge Creation.* Routledge, 2001.

Surowiecki, James. *The Wisdom of Crowds: Why the Many Are Smarter Than the Few.* Abacus, 2005.

Weinberger, David. *Small Pieces Loosely Joined: A Unified Theory of the Web.* Perseus Books, U.S., 2002.

Weinberger, David. *Everything is Miscellaneous: The Power of the New Digital Disorder.* Henry Holt & Company Inc, 2007.

ABOUT EUAN SEMPLE

Euan Semple is one of the few people in the world who can turn the complex world of the social web into something we can all understand. And, at the same time, learn how to get the most from it. Ten years ago, while working in a senior position at the BBC, Euan was one of the first to introduce what have since become known as social media tools into a large, successful organization. He has subsequently had five years of unparalleled experience working with organizations such as Nokia, The World Bank, and NATO. He is a one-man digital upgrade option for us all to download. This world is changing fast, but he makes sense of it because he understands that the core basics remain the same: community, learning, interaction. He is a master story-teller who offers a host of practical tales about how this new technology can work for real people in the real world.

INDEX

RSS (Really Simple
Syndication) 251, 270
rubbish 199–203
rules 205–9, 212–13, 215

Scoble, Robert 86
Searls, Doc 212
security issues 12, 24, 241–5
self-awareness 34–5, 37, 38, 40,
43, 255–6
self-directed systems 17, 19,
116
self-expression 7
self-reflection 34, 38, 40, 42
sense making 48
Shell 177
signal to noise ratio 75, 76–7,
78, 199, 200, 202, 203
Snowden, Dave 195, 212
Social Learn project 30
Social Media Handbook (US
Military)
206
social tools 7, 268–9
bosses' views on 64, 66, 67–8
creativity 152, 154–5, 156
crisis management 236–7,
239
encouragement of literacy
45, 46, 49
fears about 242
flexible approach to change
110
friends 92
guidelines 208
incremental approach 218
innovation 158–9
IT departments' resistance
to 11
learning from 30, 32
making sense of the world
through 172
marketing 146, 149
messiness 197
personal nature of 6, 8
recruitment 164, 165
return on investment 184

self-improvement 64–5
strategy 177–8, 179
uncertainty 169, 170, 218–19
see also blogging; forums;
wikis
Socrates 40
standards 212
strategy 11, 170, 171, 173,
175–9, 219
students 258
Surowiecki, James 160

tactical approach 172, 173
teams, self-directing 17
technology 9–13, 220
traces, leaving 21–5
training 28, 29, 31, 36–7
transparency 6, 164, 247–51
see also openness
"Trojan Mice" 12, 217–22
trolls 223–8
trust
collaboration 133
credibility 230
customers 148
inside/outside transition 143
networks 80
security issues 244, 245
shared paths 36
transparency 250
Twain, Mark 41
Twitter/tweeting
changing ecology 12
constructive dialogue 131
crisis management 237, 238
dealing with criticism 232
description of 270
globally distributed
conversations 104
interesting material 77, 78
lack of business model 182
links 47
location data 137
number of contacts on 98
observation skills 46
pompous criticism of 189
resistance to 201

281